Stephen C. Lundin, the Big Tuna Ph.D., is a writer, filmmaker and public speaker. He serves as head counsellor of the popular FISH! camps.

John Christensen is a filmmaker and CEO of ChartHouse Learning, the leading producer of corporate learning programmes, including FISH!, the video.

Harry Paul, a professional speaker, is a consulting partner with the Ken Blanchard Companies and the director of speaker services at Neslon Motivation.

Philip Strand is senior writer at ChartHouse Learning, where he helps create books, learning curriculums and mischief.

A Remarkable Way to Boost Morale and Improve Results

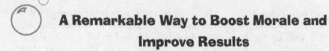

OMNIBUS

**Stephen C. Lundin, Ph.D., Harry Paul, and
John Christensen, with Philip Strand**

HODDER

MOBIUS

Hodder & Stoughton

Grateful acknowledgement is made for permission to reprint copyrighted material from the following: *Simple Abundance: A Daybook of Comfort and Joy*, copyright © 1995 by Sarah Ban Breathnach, published by Warner Books. Reprinted by permission of the author; "Faith" from *Where Many Rivers Meet: Poems*, copyright © 1996 by David Whyte, published by Many Rivers Press. Reprinted by permission of the publisher.

First published in Great Britain in 2006 by Hodder and Stoughton
A division of Hodder Headline

A Mobius paperback

18

A CIP catalogue record for this title is available from the British Library

ISBN 978-0-340-92458-7

Typeset in Granjon by Palimpsest Book Production Limited, Polmont, Stirlingshire
Printed and bound in Great Britain by
Clays Ltd, St Ives plc

Hodder Headline's policy is to use papers that are natural, renewable and recyclable products and made from wood grown in sustainable forests. The logging and manufacturing processes are expected to conform to the environmental regulations of the country of origin.

Hodder and Stoughton
A division of Hodder Headline
338 Euston Road
London NW1 3BH

This book is for the millions of workers who relish the thought of having a more playfully productive atmosphere at work and for the billions of fish who would rather not find themselves flying through the air at the world famous Pike Place Fish Market.

Enclosed are the keys to creating an innovative and accountable work environment where a playful, attentive, and engaging attitude leads to more energy, enthusiasm, productivity and creativity.

FOREWORD

by Ken Blanchard, Ph.D.,
co-author of *The One Minute Manager*,
Raving Fans, and *Gung Ho!*

Fish! is an incredible story that John Christensen first caught on film. He and his company, ChartHouse, produced an amazing video on the world famous Pike Place Fish market in Seattle. I have been showing this video at every one of my seminars to illustrate what happens when you create *Gung Ho!* employees—you ignite your workforce and create *Raving Fans®*.

Now Stephen Lundin, and long-term colleague of mine Harry Paul, have teamed up with John to bring the *Fish!* story to print. In whatever media it appears, it's a fabulous love story. As the book suggests, "When we choose to love the work we do, we can catch our limit of happiness, meaning, and fulfillment every day,"

How important is that? Incredibly important, especially when you consider that people spend about 75 percent of their adult wake time doing work-related activities—getting ready for work, traveling to work, working, contemplating work, and decompressing after work. If we spend that much time in that part of our lives, we ought to enjoy it and be energized by it. And yet, too many people are trading time on the job to satisfy needs elsewhere; "Thank God It's Friday" is still a way of life for many people.

Those days can stop now—if you read *Fish!*, share it with everyone with whom you work, and implement the four secrets and suggested strategies that Lundin, Paul, and Christensen give you. I guarantee that every manager will benefit from *Fish!*, because it will not only increase employee retention, it will motivate people to take pride in what they do. People like to work in an environment that is fun, energizing, and where they can make a difference. The *Fish!* philosophy will also benefit every employee, because it prevents burnout and will keep you excited about what you do.

As you can tell, I'm excited about *Fish!* I think this is a marvelous book. The story of the world famous Pike Place Fish market is fantastic. But this book is not just about selling fish; it's a love story that can happen in your organization, too.

FiSH!™

OMNIBUS

❧Seattle–Monday Morning

It was a wet, cold, dark, dreary, dismal Monday in Seattle, inside and out. The best the meteorologist on Channel 4 could offer was a possible break in the clouds around noon. On days like this Mary Jane Ramirez missed Southern California.

What a roller coaster, she thought, as her mind retraced the last three years. Dan, her husband, had received a great offer from Microrule and she had been confident she could find a job once they relocated. In

FISH!

just four short weeks they had given notice, packed, moved, and found great daycare for the kids. Their house hit the Los Angeles housing market just at the right time and sold immediately. True to her confidence, Mary Jane quickly found a supervisory position in the operations area of First Guarantee Financial, one of Seattle's largest financial institutions.

Dan really loved his job at Microrule. When he came home at night he was bursting with energy and full of stories about the great company for which he now worked and the advanced work they were doing. Dan and Mary Jane would frequently put the children to bed and talk well into the evening. As excited as Dan was about his new company, he was always just as interested in her day, wanting to know about her new colleagues and the challenges she was facing in her work life. Anyone watching would easily guess that they were best friends. The spirit of each shined in the presence of the other.

Their detailed planning had anticipated every possible contingency but one. Twelve months after moving to Seattle, Dan was rushed to the hospital with a burst aneurysm—"a genetic oddity" they called it—and he died of internal bleeding while never regaining consciousness. There was no warning and no time to say good-bye.

That was two years ago this month. We weren't even in Seattle a full year.

Stopping in mid–thought, with memories flooding her mind, a surge of emotion welled up inside her. She caught herself. *This is not the time to think about my personal life; the workday is less than half over, and I'm swamped with work.*

First Guarantee Financial

During her three years at First Guarantee, Mary Jane had developed a great reputation as a "can-do" supervisor. She wasn't the first to arrive or the last to leave, but she had a work ethic that almost always left her in-basket empty. The thoughtful way she conducted her work actually led to a small problem in the organization as others tried to make sure that their work passed through her part of the organization. They knew the work would get done on time and with the highest quality.

She was also a good person to work for. She always listened closely to the concerns and ideas of her staff and was well liked and respected in return. It wasn't uncommon for her to cover for someone with a sick child or important appointment. And, as a working manager, she led her department in production. She did this in an easygoing way, which rarely generated any tension—other than tension to get the job done well. Her direct reports and associates enjoyed working with and for her. Mary Jane's small group developed a reputation as a team you could count on.

In sharp contrast, there was a large operations group on the third floor that was often the topic of conversation for the opposite reason. Words like *unresponsive, entitlement, zombie, unpleasant, slow, wasteland,* and *negative* were used frequently to describe this group. It was the group everyone loved to hate. Unfortunately for the company, nearly every department needed to interact with the third floor since they processed most of First Guarantee's transactions. Everyone dreaded any contact with the operations group.

Supervisors swapped stories about the latest fiasco on the third floor. Those who visited the third floor described it as a place so dead that it sucked the life right out of you. Mary Jane remembered the laughter when one of the other managers said that he deserved a

Nobel Prize. When she asked what he meant, he said, "I think I may have discovered life on the third floor." Everyone roared.

Then, a few weeks later, Mary Jane had cautiously and somewhat reluctantly accepted a promotion to manager of the operations group on the third floor of First Guarantee. While the company had great hopes for her, she had major reservations about accepting the job. She had been comfortable in her present job—and her willingness to take risks had been much higher before Dan's death. The group she had been supervising had been with her during the rough days after Dan's death, and she had felt a strong bond with them. It would be hard to leave people who had shared so much of themselves during such dark times.

Mary Jane was acutely aware of the terrible reputation of the third floor. In fact, if it hadn't been for all of the unforeseen expenses of Dan's hospitalization, she probably would have turned down the promotion and pay raise. So here she was, on the infamous third floor. The third person to have the job in the last two years.

The Third Floor

In her first five weeks on the job she had struggled to understand the work and the people. While mildly surprised that she liked many of the people who worked on three, she quickly realized that the third floor deserved its reputation. She had observed Bob, a five-year veteran on the third floor, letting the phone ring seven times before purposely breaking the connection by unplugging the cord. She had overheard Martha describing how she handled those in the company who "hassled" her to do her processing faster—she put their file under the out-basket "by mistake." Every time Mary Jane went into the break room there was someone dozing at the table.

Most mornings the phones rang unanswered for ten to fifteen minutes after the official start of the day because the staff was still arriving. When questioned, the excuses were both abundant and lame. Everything was slow motion. The "zombie" description of the third floor was definitely deserved. Mary Jane did not have a clue what to do, only the knowledge and conviction that she must do something and do it soon.

The night before, after the kids were asleep, she had tried to work out her situation by writing in her journal. She looked down at last night's entry:

It may have been cold and dreary outside on Friday, but the view from my internal office window made dreary sound like a compliment. There was no energy there. At times I find it hard to believe there are living human beings on three. It takes a baby shower or a wedding for anyone to come alive. They never get excited about anything that's actually happening at work.

I have thirty employees for whom I am responsible and for the most part they do a slow, short day's work for a low day's pay. Many of them have done the same slow day's work in the same way for years and are totally bored. They seem to be good people, but whatever spark they may have once had, they have lost. The culture of the department is such a powerful and depressing force that new people quickly lose their spark as well. When I walk among the cubicles it feels like all the oxygen has been sucked right out of the air. I can hardly breathe.

Last week I discovered four clerks who were still not using the computer system installed here two years ago. They said they liked doing it the old way. I wonder how many other surprises are in store for me.

I suppose many back room operations are like this. Not much here to get excited about, just lots of transactions which need to be processed. But it doesn't have to be like this. I must find a way to convey how crucial our work is to the company. Our work allows others to serve the company's customers.

Although our work may be a critical part of the big picture, it happens behind the scenes and is basically taken for granted. It's an invisible part of the organization and would never appear on the company's radar screen if it wasn't so bad. And believe me, it is bad.

It is not a love for this work which brings any of us to this department. I'm not the only person with money problems on this floor. Many of the women and one of the men are also single parents. Jack's ailing

*father just moved in with him. Bonnie and her
husband now have two grandchildren as full-time
residents. The big three are why we are here: salary,
security, and benefits.*

Mary Jane pondered the last sentence she had written in her journal. Back room operations had always been lifetime positions. The pay was adequate, and the jobs were secure. Looking at the rows of cubicles and desks outside her office, she formulated some questions. "Does my staff know that the security they cherish might be just an illusion? Do they realize the extent to which market forces are reshaping this industry? Do they understand that we will all need to change in order for this company to compete in a rapidly consolidating financial services market? Are they aware that if we don't change we will eventually find ourselves looking for other employment?"

She knew the answers. No. No. No. No. Her staff members were set in their ways. They had been left alone in the back room far too long. They were just doing their jobs and hoping that retirement would come before change. And what about herself? Was her view that different?

The ringing phone pulled her back into the present. The call was followed by a sixty-minute blur of "fire fighting." First, she found out that an important client file was missing and it was rumored to have last been seen on the third floor. Next, someone from another department was so sick and tired of being put on hold she came to the third floor in person and was creating an unpleasant scene. At least there was some energy to work with. Then someone from legal was disconnected three times in a row. And one of the many staff members out ill today had an important project due. After the last fire of the morning was extinguished, Mary Jane reached for her lunch and headed for the door.

The Toxic Energy Dump

Mary Jane had begun leaving the building for lunch during the last five weeks. She knew the cafeteria lunch group would be doing what they always did, discussing the sins of the company and moaning about the third floor. It was now too personal and much too depressing to listen to their complaints. She needed some fresh air.

Most of the time she strolled down the hill to eat lunch at the waterfront. There, while nibbling on a bagel, she would gaze at the water or watch the tourists mill around the little shops. It was a tranquil setting, and Puget Sound provided her some contact with the natural world.

She had only made it two cubicles from her office when she heard the distinct sound of her phone ringing. *It could be the day care*, she thought. *Stacy did have a runny nose this morning.* So she raced back to her office, picking up the phone on the fourth ring. "This is Mary Jane Ramirez," she gasped.

"Mary Jane, this is Bill."

Oh boy, what now, she wondered, as she listened to the voice of her new boss. Bill was another reason she had thought twice about taking the job on three. He had a reputation as a real SOB. As far as she could tell, his reputation was deserved. He would issue commands, cut you off midsentence, and he had an annoying habit of asking about the status of projects in a paternal way. "Mary Jane, are you staying on top of the Stanton project?" As if she didn't have a clue. Mary

Jane was the third manager in two years, and she was beginning to understand that it wasn't just the problems with the people on three, it was also Bill.

"I've just come out of an all-morning meeting with the leadership group, and I want to meet with you this afternoon."

"Sure, Bill, is there a problem?"

"The leadership is convinced that we're in for some tough times and in order to survive, we will need the best from everyone. More productivity from the same employees, or we start making changes. We talked about the corrosive effect of a few departments, where the energy and morale are so low that it pulls everyone down."

A feeling of dread descended upon Mary Jane.

"The boss went to one of those touchy-feely conferences on spirit in the workplace, and he's all fired up. I don't think it's fair to single out the third floor, but he seems to believe the third floor is the biggest problem."

"He singled out the third floor?"

"Not only did he single out the third floor, but he had a special name for it. He called it a 'toxic energy dump.' I don't want one of my departments called a toxic energy dump! It's unacceptable! It's embarrassing."

"A toxic energy dump?"

"Yes. And the boss really grilled me on what I'm doing about it. I told him I shared his concern and that I brought you in to solve the problem. He told me he wants to be kept informed of the progress. So, have you solved it yet?"

Had she solved it yet?! She only took the job five weeks ago! "Not yet," she said.

"Well, you have to speed things up, Mary Jane. If you're not up to it I need to know so I can make the appropriate changes. The boss is absolutely convinced we all need more energy, passion, and spirit on the job. I'm not sure why the third floor needs passion and energy. The stuff you do there is not rocket science. Personally, I've never expected a lot from a bunch of clerks. I guess the third floor has been the butt of jokes for so long that he thinks if we fix it, we solve the problem. What time can you meet?"

"How about two o'clock, Bill?"

"Two-thirty, OK?"

"Sure."

Bill must have heard the frustration in her voice. "Now don't get upset, Mary Jane. You just get to work on this."

He really is hard to take, she thought as she hung up the phone. *Don't get upset! He is my boss, and the problem is real. But what a jerk.*

A Change in Routine

Mary Jane's mind was ablaze as she moved toward the elevators a second time. Rather than heading down the hill to the waterfront as usual, she impulsively turned right on First Street, thinking she needed a longer walk. The words *toxic energy dump* played over and over in her head.

Toxic energy dump! What next? She was walking along First Street when a small voice inside her head whispered, "The toxic energy is what you hate most about the third floor. Something needs to happen."

Mary Jane's impulsive stroll down First Street took her to a part of town that was new to her. Sounds of pealing laughter caught her attention and she was surprised to see the public market to her left. She had heard about it, but with her tight financial situation and two young children, she usually avoided specialty markets. With her need to live frugally until the medical bills were paid in full, it was just easier to stay away. She had driven through the area but had never been there on foot.

As she turned and walked down Pike Place, she saw that a large crowd of well-dressed people was clustered around one of the fish markets, and everyone was laughing. At first she felt herself resisting the laughter, dwelling on the seriousness of her predicament. She almost turned away. Then a voice in her head said, "I could use a good laugh," and she moved closer. One of the fish guys yelled out, "Good afternoon, yogurt dudes!" Dozens of well-dressed people then hoisted yogurt cups into the air. *My goodness*, she thought. *What have I stumbled upon?*

The world famous Pike Place Fish market

Was that a fish flying through the air? She wondered if her eyes were playing tricks on her; then it happened again. One of the workers—they were distinctive in their white aprons and black rubber boots—picked up a large fish, threw it twenty feet to the raised counter, and shouted, "One salmon flying away to Minnesota." Then all the other workers repeated in unison, "One salmon flying away to Minnesota." The guy behind the counter made an unbelievable one-handed catch, then bowed his head to the people applauding his skill. The energy was remarkable.

To her right, another worker was playfully teasing a small boy by making a large fish move its mouth as if it were talking. A slightly older fish guy with thinning gray hair was walking around shouting, "Questions, questions, answers to any questions about fish!" A young worker at the cash register was juggling crabs. Two card-carrying members of AARP were laughing uncontrollably as their fish guy salesman carried on a conversation with the fish they had chosen. The place was wild. She could feel herself relax as she enjoyed the spectacle.

She looked at the people holding the yogurt cups in the air and thought, *Office workers. Do they really buy fish at lunch or do they just come to watch the action?*

Mary Jane was unaware that one of the fish guys had noticed her in the crowd. There was something about her curiosity and seriousness which caused him to walk over.

"What's the matter? Don't you have any yogurt?" She looked around and saw a handsome young man with long curly black hair. He was looking at her intently, a big smile on his face.

"I have yogurt in the bag," she stammered as she gestured to her brown bag, "but I'm not sure what is happening."

"Have you been here before?"

"No. I usually go down to the waterfront for lunch."

"I can understand that—it's peaceful by the water. Not very peaceful here, that's for sure. So what brings you here today?"

Off to her right one of the fish guys, looking lost, was shouting, "Who wants to buy a fish?" Another was teasing a young woman. A crab sailed over Mary Jane's head. "Six crabs flying away to Montana," someone shouted. "Six crabs flying away to Montana," they all repeated. A fish guy wearing a wool cap was dancing behind the cash register. It was a controlled madhouse all around her, like the rides at the state fair, only better. But the fish guy at her side didn't seem at all distracted. He was pleasantly and patiently waiting for her response. *My goodness*, she thought. *He actually seems interested in my answer. But I'm not going to tell a total stranger about my troubles at work.* Then she did just that.

His name was Lonnie, and he listened attentively to her description of the third floor. He didn't flinch when one of the flying fish hit a rope and smacked the ground right beside them. He listened closely as she described the many employee problems she had identified. When she finished telling her story, she looked at Lonnie and asked, "So what do you think about my toxic energy dump?"

"That's quite a story. I've worked in some pretty dreary places myself. In fact this place used to be pretty crappy. What do you notice about the market now?"

"The noise, the action, the energy," she said, without a moment's hesitation.

"And how do you like all this energy?"

"I love it," she replied. "I really love it!"

"Me, too. I'm spoiled for life. I don't think I could work in a typical market after experiencing this. As I mentioned, the market didn't start this way. It, too, was an energy dump for many years. Then we decided to change things—and this is the result. Would energy like this make a difference with your group?"

"It sure would. It's what we need at the dump," she said, smiling.

"I'd be happy to describe what I think makes this fish market different. Who knows, you might get some ideas."

"But, but we don't have anything to throw! We have boring work to do. Most of us . . ."

"Slow down. It's not just about throwing fish. Of course your business is different, and it sounds like you have a serious challenge facing you. I'd like to help. What if you could find your own way to apply some of the lessons we learned while becoming the world famous Pike Place Fish market? Wouldn't the possibility of an energized department make it worthwhile for you to learn those lessons?"

"Yes. For sure! But why would you do this for me?"

"Being a part of this little fish market community and experiencing what you see here has made a big difference in my life. I won't bore you with the personal details, but my life was a real mess when I took this job. Working here has literally saved my life. It may sound a little sappy, but I believe I have an obligation to seek out and find ways to demonstrate my gratitude for this life I enjoy. You made that easy for me by telling me about your problem. I really believe you can find some of your answers here. We've created a lot of great energy." As he said the word *energy*, a crab sailed by and someone shouted with a Texas twang, "Five crabs flying away to Wisconsin." A chorus echoed, "Five crabs flying away to Wisconsin."

"Fair enough," she answered, laughing out loud. "If the fish market has anything, it has energy. It's a deal." She looked at her watch and realized she would have to walk fast in order to get back to work within the lunch hour. She had no doubt her arrivals and departures were being clocked by her staff.

Lonnie caught her glance and said, "Hey, why don't you come back for your lunch break tomorrow— and bring *two* yogurts."

He turned and immediately began helping a young man in a Vikings jacket understand the difference between a Copper River salmon and a King salmon.

Return Visit

At lunchtime on Tuesday she walked quickly down First Street to the market. Lonnie must have been watching for her; he immediately emerged from the crowd and directed her down a ramp past the T-shirt concession.

"There are some tables at the end of the hall," he said, and led the way to a small glass-enclosed room with a great view of the harbor and Puget Sound. Lonnie ate a bagel and the yogurt Mary Jane brought him while she ate her yogurt and asked about the workings of a fish market. Fishmongering really didn't sound very appealing after Lonnie told her about a typical day; this made the attitude of the workers at the Pike Place Fish market all the more impressive.

"It would seem that your work and my work have more in common than I thought," she said, after Lonnie described the tedious tasks that needed to be conducted each day.

Lonnie looked up, "Really?"

"Yes, most of the work my staff does can be mundane and repetitious, to say the least. It's important work, however. We never see a customer, but if we make a mistake, the customer is upset and we receive a lot of criticism. If we do our work well, no one notices. In general, the work is boring. You've taken boring work and made the way you do the work interesting. I find that fascinating."

"Have you ever considered the fact that any work can be boring to the person who has to do it? Some of the yogurt dudes travel all over the world for business. It sounds pretty exciting to me, but they tell me it gets old fast. I guess given the right conditions, any job can be dull."

"I agree with what you said. When I was a teenager I had a chance to do a job many teenage girls often dream about: I received a modeling contract. But by the end of the first month I was bored to tears. It was almost all just standing around, waiting. Or take newscasters. I've since learned that many do nothing other than read other people's text. That sounds boring, also—at least to me."

"OK. If we agree that any job can be boring, can we agree that any job can be performed with energy and enthusiasm?"

"I'm not sure. Can you give me an example?"

"That's easy. Walk around the market and look at the other fish shops. They don't get it. They are, what was the phrase you used . . . toxic energy dumps. The way they approach their work is really good for *our* business. I've told you the Pike Place Fish market used to be like them. Then we discovered an amazing thing. *There is always a choice about the way you do your work, even if there is not a choice about the work itself.* That was the biggest lesson we learned in building the world famous Pike Place Fish market. *We can choose the attitude we bring to our work.*"

CHOOSE YOUR ATTITUDE

Mary Jane pulled out a notepad and began writing:

**There is always a choice about
the way you do your work,
even if there is not
a choice about the work itself.**

Then she thought about the words she had just written, and asked, "Why wouldn't you have a choice about the work itself?"

"Good point. You can always quit your job, and so in that sense you have a choice about the work you do. But it might not be a smart thing to do given your responsibilities and other factors. That's what I mean by choice. On the other hand, you always have a choice about the attitude you bring to the job."

Lonnie continued, "Let me tell you about my grandmother. She always brought love and a smile to her work. All of us grandkids wanted to help in the kitchen because washing dishes with Grandma was so much fun. In the process a great deal of kitchen wisdom was dispensed. Us kids were given something truly precious, a caring adult.

"I realize now that my grandmother didn't love dishwashing. She *brought* love to dishwashing, and her spirit was infectious.

"Likewise, my buddies and I realized that each day when we come to the fish market we bring an attitude. We can bring a moody attitude and have a depressing day. We can bring a grouchy attitude and irritate our coworkers and customers. Or we can bring a sunny, playful, cheerful attitude and have a great day. We can choose the kind of day we will have. We spent a lot of time talking about this choice, and we realized that as long as we are going to be at work, we might as well have the best day we can have. Make sense to you?"

"It sure does."

"In fact, we got so excited about our choices that we also chose to be world famous. A day spent 'being world famous' is a lot more enjoyable than a day spent being ordinary. Do you see what I am saying? Working in a fish market is cold, wet, smelly, sloppy, difficult work. But we have a choice about our attitude while we are doing that work."

"Yes, I think I get it. You choose the attitude you

bring to work each day. That choice determines the way you are at work. As long as you are here, why not choose to be world famous rather than ordinary? It seems so simple."

"Simple to understand, but more difficult to do. We didn't create this place overnight; it took almost a year. I was a hard case myself—you might say I used to have a chip on my shoulder. My personal life was kind of out of control as well. I really never thought much about it, just assumed I knew how life worked. Life was tough, and I responded in kind—I was tough. Then when we decided to create a different kind of fish market, I resisted the notion that I could choose how I lived each day. I had too much invested in being a victim. One of the older guys, who also had been through some tough times, took me aside and explained it to me, one monger to another. I did some soul searching and decided I would give it a try. I've become a believer. A person can choose their attitude. I know that because I chose mine."

Mary Jane found herself impressed with what she was hearing and also with the person from whom she was hearing it. She looked up to find Lonnie eyeing her quizzically and realized she had been daydreaming.

"Sorry. I'll give it a try. What else explains your success here?"

"There are four ingredients, but this one is the core. Without choosing your attitude the others are a waste of time. So let's stop here and save the other three for later. Take the first ingredient and see what you can do with it back on the third floor. Call me when you're ready to discuss the rest. Do you have our number?"

"It's written everywhere in the shop!"

"Oh yeah. We aren't shy, are we? See you later. And thanks for the yogurt."

The Courage to Change

The demands of her job kept Mary Jane on a treadmill of activity for the next two days. That was her excuse, anyway. But her thoughts were often on her conversation with Lonnie and the idea of choosing the attitude you bring to work. She realized that even though she agreed with the philosophy of the fish market, there was something holding her back. *When in doubt, get more data*, she thought.

On Friday, she decided to ask Bill about the conference his boss had attended, the one about spirit in the workplace. It might be wise to learn more about his experience. That afternoon, she called Bill.

"Bill, how can I get up to speed on the spirit in the workplace conference the big guy attended?"

"What do you want to do that for? It was one of those 'new age' deals. They probably spent most of their time in hot tubs. Why do you want to waste your time on that?"

Mary Jane felt herself getting angry. She took a deep breath. "Look, Bill, when I took this job we both knew there was a lot to do. Now the stakes are higher, and the timeline is shorter. You are in this as deep as I am. Are you going to help me or give me a hard time?"

I can't believe I said that, she thought. *But it sure felt good!*

Bill responded evenly; this confrontational approach actually seemed to make him more comfortable. "OK, OK. Don't get all worked up. I have an audio tape from the conference on my desk that I'm supposed to listen to. I just haven't had time. You take it and fill me in?"

"Sure, Bill. I'll come by and pick it up."

A Memorable Commute

The commute to Bellevue was bumper to bumper, but Mary Jane didn't notice. She was mulling over her situation. *When did I lose my confidence?* she wondered to herself. *Speaking up to Bill is the first courageous thing I have done in a long time. Two years to be exact*, she realized, as she finally started putting the pieces together at the edge of her consciousness. *Too much to think about.* Feeling overwhelmed, she put Bill's tape into the cassette player.

From the car stereo speakers came a deep, resonant voice that was mesmerizing. The tape was a recording of verse from a poet who took his poetry to the workplace, believing the language of poetry could help us cope with the issues of the day. His name was David Whyte. He would talk a while and then recite a poem. His poems and stories washed over her. Phrases jumped out at her.

> The needs of the organization and our needs as workers are the same. Creativity, passion, flexibility, wholeheartedness . . .

Yes, she thought.

FISH!

We crack the windows of our cars in the corporate parking lot in the summer, not to save the upholstery from the heat, but because only sixty percent of us goes into that place, and the rest of us stays in the car all day and must breathe out there. What would it be like to take our whole self to work?

Who is this guy? Then without warning, she filled with emotion as she heard David Whyte recite his poem *Faith*. He introduced it to his audience by saying he wrote it at a time when he had very little faith himself:

Faith

BY DAVID WHYTE

I want to write about faith
about the way the moon rises
over cold snow, night after night

faithful even as it fades from fullness
slowly becoming that last curving and impossible
sliver of light before the final darkness
but I have no faith myself
I refuse to give it the smallest entry

Let this then, my small poem,
like a new moon, slender and barely open,
be the first prayer that opens me to faith

So this is what is meant by the statement, "When the student is ready the teacher appears." The poem had created a moment of insight, and Mary Jane finally saw what was holding her back. With Dan's sudden death and the pressures of being a responsible single mom, she had lost faith in her ability to survive in the world. She was afraid that if she took a risk and failed, she would not be able to support herself and her children.

Leading a change at work would be risky. She could fail and lose her job. That was a distinct possibility. Then she thought about the risk of not changing. *If we don't change, we could all lose our jobs. Not only that: I don't want to work in a place with no energy or life. I know what it will do to me over time, and the picture is not pretty. What kind of a mother would I be if I let that happen? What example would I set? If I launch the change process on Monday, the first step must be for me to choose* my *attitude. I choose faith. I must trust that whatever happens I will be all right.*

I'm a survivor; I've proven that. I will be all right, whatever happens. It's time to clean up the toxic energy dump. Not just because it would be good for business—although I believe it will be great for business. And not just because I have been challenged to solve the problem—that is an important reason, but it's an external issue. The compelling reason to move ahead comes from my inside. I need to renew my faith in myself; tackling this problem will help me do just that.

She remembered some lines from the tape: "I don't believe that companies are necessarily prisons, but sometimes we make prisons of them by the way we choose to work there. I have created a prison and the walls are my own lack of faith in myself."

The prison metaphor had a familiar ring—she was sure she had encountered it before in a seminar she had attended. As soon as she arrived at the daycare, she parked her car, took out her journal, and wrote:

Life is too precious to spend any time at all, much less half of my waking hours, in a toxic energy dump. I don't want to live like that, and I am sure my associates will feel the same way once they have a recognizable choice.

The culture in my department has been the way it is for a long time. In order to change the culture, I will need to take personal risks with no assurance of success. This could be a blessing. Recent events have shaken my faith in myself and taking the necessary risks could help me renew my faith. The fact is that the risk of doing nothing is probably greater than the risk of acting.

Somewhere in my files is material which contains a message that could be timely. I need to find that message because I need all the help I can get.

With that she got out of the car and went in to pick up her daughter.

"Mommy, Mommy. Your eyes are wet. Have you been crying? What's wrong, Mommy?"

"Yes, sweetheart, I've been crying, but it was good crying. How was your day?"

"I made a picture of our family, do you want to see it?"

"I sure do." She looked down and saw the four figures her daughter had drawn, looking back at her. "Oh boy," she exhaled. *Another test of faith.*

"Get your things honey; we have to go pick up Brad."

Sunday Afternoon

Sunday afternoon was Mom's time. Mary Jane arranged to have a sitter for at least two hours every Sunday. It was a little reward she gave herself, one which always left her refreshed and ready for the challenges of work and family. She used the time to read inspirational material or a good novel, go for a bike ride, or just sip coffee and relax. Seattle was full of coffee shops and there was a great spot three blocks away. She grabbed some books and headed out. Her favorite table in a private corner of the shop was waiting for her.

"Grande skinny latte please." She sat down with her latte and decided to start with some inspirational reading. She pulled out her tattered copy of Sarah Ban Breathnach's *Simple Abundance*, a book which contains a reading for every day of the year, and turned to February 8. Key words seemed to jump off the page:

> Most of us are uncomfortable thinking of ourselves as artists . . . But each of us is an artist . . . With every *choice*, every day, you are *creating* a unique work of art. Something that only you can do . . . The reason you were born was to leave your own indelible mark on the world.

This is your *authenticity* . . . *Respect* your creative urges . . . step out in *faith* . . . you will discover your *choices* are as authentic as you are. What is more, you will discover that your life is all it was meant to be: a joyous sonnet of thanksgiving.

She had planned on thinking a little bit about work, and the words about choice and faith took her back to the fish market. *Those guys are artists*, she thought, *and they must choose to create each day*. And she had a startling thought: *I can be an artist, too*.

Then, she took out a file from a leadership seminar she had attended. This was where she first heard prison being used as a metaphor for work. Inside was a faded photocopy of a speech written by John Gardner. She recalled that Gardner encouraged people to reproduce his papers, a generous gesture, she thought. *He must have said something powerful if I remember him after all this time*. She searched through the speech, page by page.

FISH!

The Writing of John Gardner

The passage began:

> There is the puzzle of why some men and women go to seed, while others remain vital to the very end of their days. Going to seed may be too vague an expression. Perhaps I should say that many people, somewhere along the line, stop learning and growing.

Mary Jane looked up as she thought, *That fits my group. And it fits the old me, as well.* She smiled at the decision implied by "the old me." She went back to the passage:

> One must be compassionate in assessing the reasons. Perhaps life just presented them with tougher problems than they could solve. Perhaps something inflicted a major wound to their self-confidence or their self-esteem . . . Or maybe they just ran so hard for so long that they forgot what they were running for.
>
> I'm talking about people who, no matter

how busy they may seem, have stopped learning and growing. I don't deride that. Life is hard. Sometimes just to keep on keeping on is an act of courage . . .

We have to face the fact that most men and women out there in the world of work are more stale than they know, more bored than they would care to admit . . .

A famous French writer said, "There are people whose clocks stop at a certain point in their lives." I've watched a lot of people move through life. As Yogi Berra says, "You can observe a lot by watching." *I am convinced that most people enjoy learning and growing, at any time in their life.* If we are aware of the danger of going to seed we can take countervailing measures. If your clock is unwound you can wind it up again.

There is something I know about you that you may not even know about yourself. You have within you more resources of energy than have ever been tapped, more talent than has ever been exploited, more strength than has ever been tested, and more to give than you have ever given.

No wonder I remember John Gardner. I have a lot of clocks to wind up, but first I need to wind up my own, she thought.

For the next hour Mary Jane wrote in her journal and was pleased to note that she had become quite peaceful. As she prepared to return home, she looked over what she had written and circled the section that would be her guide on Monday morning.

Solving the problem of the toxic energy dump will require me to become a leader in every sense of the word. I will need to risk the possibility of failure. There is no safe harbor. But to take no action is to fail for sure. I might as well get started. My first step is to choose my attitude. I choose confidence, trust, and faith. I will wind up my clock and get ready to enjoy learning and growing as I work to apply the lessons from the fish market to my toxic energy dump.

Monday Morning

At 5:30 A.M. she felt some pangs of guilt as she sat outside her daughter's daycare center, waiting for the
doors to open. On rare days like this, Brad would also
stay at the daycare until a bus took him to school. She
looked over at the sleepy-eyed kids and said, "I won't
get you out of bed so early very often kids, but today I
need to get to the office to prepare for a really important project."

Brad rubbed his eyes and said, "That's all right,
Mom." Then Stacy piped up, "Yeah, it's fun to get here
first. We get first pick of video games!"

When the doors opened, Mary Jane signed them in
and gave them each a big hug. When she looked back
they were already busy.

It was an easy commute; by 5:55, she was at her
desk with a steaming cup of coffee and a pad. She took
out a pen and wrote in large letters:

CHOOSE YOUR ATTITUDE

Steps:
- Call a meeting and speak from the heart.
- Find a message that communicates the notion of choosing your attitude in a way that everyone will understand and personalize.
- Provide motivation.
- Persist with faith.

Now the tough part. What do I say to my staff here on three? And she began writing down her thoughts.

On Monday mornings the staff met in two shifts; one group covered the phones while the other met with her in the conference room—then they switched. As the first group assembled, she listened to the discussions of family activity and the universal complaints about Monday morning. *These are good people*, she thought; she felt her heart beating faster as they quieted and turned their attention to her. *Here goes everything.*

Mary Jane's Presentation

"Today we have a serious issue to discuss. A couple of weeks ago the group vice president went to a conference and returned convinced that First Guarantee needs to become a place that is more energetic and enthusiastic. He is convinced that energy and enthusiasm are the keys to productivity, successful recruitment, long-term retention, great customer service, and a host of other qualities that we need in order to compete in our changing and consolidating business. He called a meeting of the leadership group—and at that meeting he referred to the third floor as a 'toxic energy dump.' That's right, he called our floor a toxic energy dump and said it needed to be cleaned."

Mary Jane looked at the startled expressions. A comment came quickly from Adam, a long-term employee: "I'd like to see them do this work. It's the most boring work on earth."

Then one of the least energetic employees said, "What difference does it make if there is energy here? We get the work done, don't we?"

No one challenged the accusation that their energy was toxic.

Mary Jane continued, "I want you to know that this issue is not going away. Oh, the group VP may lose interest, and Bill might forget about it with time, but I will not. You see, I am in full agreement. We are a toxic energy dump. Other parts of the company hate dealing with us. They also call us 'the pit.' They joke about us at lunch. They laugh about us in the halls. And they are right. Heck, many of us hate coming here, and even we call this a pit. I think we can and should change that; I want you to know why."

The startled expressions were now replaced with truly stunned expressions. The silence was complete.

"You all know my story. How Dan and I came to town with our hopes, dreams, and two small children. How Dan's sudden death left me alone. How Dan's insurance didn't cover many of the big expenses. How I found myself in a difficult financial position.

"What you may not know is how all this affected me. Some of you are single moms and dads and know what I am talking about. I needed this job, and I had lost my confidence. I went with the flow, never doing anything that could threaten my security. It seems funny that my security is now threatened and it may be because I went with the flow. Well, those days are over.

"Here is the bottom line. I still need this job, but I don't want to spend the rest of my working life in a toxic energy dump. Dan's lesson had been lost on me until now. *Life is too precious just to be passing through to retirement.* We simply spend too much time at work to allow it to be wasted. I think we can make this a better place to work.

"Now the good news. I know a consultant who works for a world famous organization and is an expert on energy. You will meet him eventually. Today I am going to convey his first bit of advice: *We choose our attitude.*"

Mary Jane continued by discussing the concept of choosing your attitude. Then she asked if there were any questions.

Steve raised his hand. When Mary Jane nodded to him, he said, "Suppose I'm driving my car and some idiot cuts me off in traffic. That causes me to get upset and I may honk or even make a gesture, if you know what I mean. What's with the choice thing? I didn't do it; it was done to me. I didn't have a choice."

"Let me ask you something, Steve. If you were in a tough part of town, would you have used that gesture?"

Steve smiled. "No way! You can get hurt doing that."

"So you can choose your response in a tough part of town, but you have no choice in the suburbs?"

"OK, Mary Jane. OK, I get it."

"You couldn't have asked a better question, Steve. We can't control the way other people drive, but we can choose how we respond. Here at First Guarantee we don't have a lot to do with selecting the work that needs to be done, but we can choose how we approach that work. I want all of you to think of ways this is true and see if you can identify things we can do to remind ourselves of our choices. Good luck. Our work life depends on it."

The second staff meeting was much like the first. When she didn't get any questions, she used Steve's question from the first group. It was 10:30 on Monday morning. She was drained from the meetings, but realized it was her first opportunity to choose her attitude. And she did.

The week sped by. She made a point of walking around the office each day and being available to talk about the idea of choosing your attitude. When she saw Steve, he said, "Boy, you really nailed me at the staff meeting."

"I hope I didn't embarrass you."

"Mary Jane, you did me a big favor. My life has been a series of reactions lately. You reminded me that I have important choices to make and that I can make them if I have a little self-control and courage."

"Courage?"

"I am in a bad relationship; I need to do something about it. I can see now that reacting and feeling like a victim is not going to solve the problem. The problem needs to be confronted. I'm sorry to be so evasive, but it is rather personal."

"Good luck, Steve, and thanks for trusting me with your story."

"Oh, we all trust you, Mary Jane. It's just that this work is so boring and all we hear are complaints. We feel like we're always under attack. Keep at it; I'm behind you all the way."

She was pleasantly surprised by the many words of encouragement. While staff members were not sure about the details, most liked the idea of creating a more satisfying work environment.

Then on Friday it happened. She walked off the elevator on the third floor and was confronted with a giant poster. On the top it said: CHOOSE YOUR ATTITUDE, and in the middle were the words: MENU CHOICES FOR THE DAY. Down below the menu were two drawings. One was a smiling face and the other was a frowning face. She was ecstatic. *They do get it!* she thought to herself and raced to her office to call Lonnie.

After telling him about the menu, she suggested they finish their discussion. Lonnie asked about lunch Monday. Mary Jane said she really didn't want to wait until next week, so they agreed she should come to the market on Saturday and bring the kids with her.

Saturday at the Fish Market

Saturdays are always busy at the market; Lonnie suggested they come early. Mary Jane foolishly asked what the earliest time was they might arrive. Lonnie said he started work at 5 A.M. They settled on 8.

Brad and Stacy got in the car drowsy, but by the time they had all made the trip into Seattle and found a parking spot, her kids were wired and ready for action. The questions were unending. "Where do they get the fish? Are they big fish? Do they have any sharks? Will there be any other kids there?"

As the three walked down Pike Place to the market, Mary Jane was struck by how quiet and calm it was. She immediately spotted Lonnie standing by the fish display. She was impressed with how neatly organized the stand was, with the fish and seafood packed in ice and signs detailing names, prices, and special qualities. One section was empty except for the ice.

"Good morning," said Lonnie with his customary smile. "And who are these two fishmongers?"

Mary Jane introduced her children. Lonnie welcomed them and said it was time to get to work. As she was removing her notepad from her purse, he stopped her and said, "No, not that kind of work. I thought you three could help me finish this display."

"Cool," said Brad.

"I couldn't find any boots your size, but I did find three aprons to wear. Here, put these on and we'll start packing fish."

Stacy looked a little bewildered; Mary Jane gave her a quick hug. Lonnie took Brad into the back of the store to visit the fish locker, while Mary Jane kept Stacy entertained with a walk among the displays. In about fifteen minutes, Lonnie and Brad returned pushing a mammoth cart full of fish. To be exact, Lonnie was pushing the cart—Brad was hanging on to the handle with his feet just touching the ground.

PLAY

"Mom! Wow! It rocks back there! There must be a million fish. Isn't that right, Lonnie? I got to help, too!" Lonnie gave him a big smile and a nod, but pretended to be all business. "We have to pack these fish so the market can open, little buddy. Ready to give me a hand?"

Brad was having a ball. He would help Lonnie pick up a tuna and Lonnie would pack it in ice, adding to a neat row of fish. The tuna were almost as big as Brad, and Mary Jane was sorry she didn't bring her camera. The way Lonnie worked with Brad was magic. Once in a while Lonnie would trick Brad, pretend the fish bit him, or do something that caused Brad to laugh. When there was room for only two more tuna in the row, Lonnie turned the job over to Brad, but provided some subtle help lifting. If Brad were asked to pick his "action hero" at that moment, he would have chosen Lonnie.

"Now it's time for your mom to get to work. Take out that notebook, Mary Jane, and Brad will give you the second ingredient of an energy-filled workplace."

"Brad?"

"You bet. The second ingredient selected by a bunch of fishmongers who choose their attitude is something that is familiar to any kid. We just forget its importance as we become older and more serious. Brad, tell your mom what you do at recess."

Brad looked over the top of the tuna that was pinning him to the edge of the counter and said, "Play."

Mary Jane opened her journal and made a new note: PLAY! Her mind flashed back to the scene at the market she witnessed on that first day. She had been looking at a playground with adult kids at recess. Throwing fish, kidding with each other and the customers, calling out orders, repeating the calls. The place had been electric.

"Don't misunderstand," said Lonnie. "This is a real business which is run to make a profit. This business pays a lot of salaries, and we take the business seriously, but we discovered we could be serious about business and still have fun with the way we conducted business. You know, not get all uptight, but let things flow. What many of our customers think of as entertainment is just a bunch of adult kids having a good time, but doing it in a respectful manner.

"And the benefits are many. We sell a lot of fish. We have low turnover. We enjoy work that *can* be very tedious. We have become great friends, like the players on a winning team. We have a lot of pride in what we do and the way we do it. And we have become world famous. All from doing something which Brad does without much thought. We know how to play!"

Brad said, "Hey, Mom, why don't you bring the people at work to Lonnie so he can teach them how to play?"

MAKE THEIR DAY

Suddenly someone addressed Mary Jane from the side. "Hey, reporter lady, want to buy a fish?" One of Lonnie's associates had come over and was holding a huge fish head in his hand. "I'll give you a great deal on this one. It's missing a few parts but the price is right." He made the fish's mouth into a smile and said, "I call it smiling sushi. Just a penny." And he looked at her with a crazy, crooked smile.

Lonnie was laughing and, of course, Brad wanted to hold it. Stacy was hiding behind Mom's legs. Mary

Jane took out a penny and gave it to the fish guy they called "Wolf." She didn't need to ask why they called him Wolf. His hair was unruly and his eyes tracked everything as if it were prey. This wolf was clearly domesticated, however, and if such a thing were possible, Wolf had a grandfatherly air about him. Wolf put the smiling sushi in a bag and gave it to Brad, who was beaming. Shy Stacy piped up for the first time that morning and said she wanted one, too. Wolf brought over two more. Now they all had a smiling sushi.

Lonnie said, "Thanks, Wolf. You just showed us the third ingredient in creating a high-energy, world famous market."

"He did?"

"Think back to the first two times you were here, Mary Jane. What stands out in your mind?"

"I remember a young redheaded woman, about twenty years old. She got up on the platform and tried to catch a fish. Of course she found them a little slippery and missed twice. But she had a ball."

"Why was that so memorable?"

"She was so animated, so alive. And the rest of us in the crowd identified with her. We could imagine ourselves in her place."

"And what do you think Brad will remember about today?"

"Doing big-guy stuff, visiting the cold fish locker, and working with you."

"We call that *make their day*. We look for as many ways as we can to create great memories. And we create great memories whenever we *make someone's day*. The playful way we do our work allows us to find creative ways to engage our customers. That's the key word: *engage*. We try not to stand apart from our customers but to find ways to respectfully include them in our fun. Respectfully. When we are successful, it makes their day."

Mary Jane opened her journal again and wrote: MAKE THEIR DAY. Her mind filled with thoughts: *They engage people and welcome them to join in the fun. Customers like being a part of the show, and memories are created here which will bring smiles and make good stories for a long time afterward. Involving others and working to "make their day" directs attention toward the customer. Great psychology. Focusing your attention on ways to make another person's day provides a constant flow of positive feelings.*

"Hello, anyone home?"

Lonnie, Brad, and Stacy were all staring at her. "Sorry, I got to thinking about how powerful an ingredient that is. I hope we can find a way to apply *make their day* at First Guarantee."

"The market is opening. Let's take the kids for something to eat; we can finish our discussion there. You kids hungry?"

"Yeah!"

BE PRESENT

They found a table at the café across the street and ordered coffee, hot chocolate, and sweet rolls. The market was rapidly filling with people, and Lonnie directed her attention to the way the fish guys interacted with those people. He asked her to watch them in action and told her she would discover the final ingredient if she watched carefully. Her eyes went from one monger to another, marveling at their playful manner and the lighthearted way they went about their work. She then turned her attention to those who were between activities. They looked vigilant, eyes roaming for the next opportunity for action.

It was actually a bad experience from the night before that helped her find the answer. She remembered her trip to the store with two cranky kids, both ready for bed. How long did she stand at the counter waiting for a clerk who was talking to another clerk about the modifications he made to his car? It seemed forever as the kids pulled on her dress with growing impatience. *That wouldn't happen here*, she thought. *These guys are present. They are fully engaged in their work. I wonder if they even daydream?* She asked Lonnie if that was the answer.

"You got it. Why am I not surprised?" He flashed his boyish grin. "Look out toxic energy dump, here she comes!" Then Lonnie continued, "I was at the grocery store, waiting my turn at the meat counter. The staff was pleasant and having a good time. The problem was they were having a good time with each other, not me. If they had included me in their fun, it would have been a whole different experience. They had most of it right but were missing the key ingredient. They weren't present and focused on me, the customer. They were internally focused."

She opened her journal and wrote: BE PRESENT.

Lonnie was showing his first sign of not being present. She knew why when he said, "I need to get back to work. The guys were more than willing to cover for me, but I don't want to overdo it. There is, however, one piece of advice I would like to offer before I leave."

"I'm all ears."

"Well, I don't mean to tell you how to do your job but I think it will be important for you to *find a way for your staff to discover the Fish Philosophy for themselves*. I'm not sure just telling them about the Fish Philosophy will do the trick. Brad had a good idea when he said you should bring them here."

"You and Brad make quite a team. In my rush to solve the problem, I could easily forget that the members of my staff need to have learning experiences of their own, and time to internalize the experience. Thanks so much—for everything. You made our day."

Brad couldn't stop talking on the way home; it was all she could do to be present for him. One somewhat crazy idea found its way into her head. She grinned and tucked it away for Monday.

> *She told me and then I*
> *discovered it for myself.*
> Unknown

Sunday Afternoon

During her private time on Sunday afternoon, Mary Jane opened her journal and briefly expanded on her notes.

CHOOSE YOUR ATTITUDE—I think we have a good start on this one. The menu idea the staff came up with was terrific; the first real sign of progress. Without choose your attitude, *all the rest is a waste of time. I need to continue exploring and expanding our awareness of this ingredient.*

PLAY—The fish market is an adult playground. If the fish guys can have that much fun selling fish, there is hope for us at First Guarantee.

MAKE THEIR DAY—Customers are encouraged to play also. The atmosphere is one of inclusion. Not at all like the boss I had in L.A. who talked to me like I was a tape recorder and never shared any of the interesting work.

BE PRESENT—The fish guys are fully present. They are not daydreaming or on the phone. They are

scanning the crowd and interacting with customers.
They talk to me as if I was a long lost friend.

Monday Morning

As she entered the elevator, she noticed Bill right behind her. *That will save me the trip to his office*, she thought. The car was crowded so they didn't converse, but when the door opened on her floor, she turned to Bill and handed her boss her bag, which had a distinct odor emanating from it. "A gift, Bill. It's called a smiling sushi." As the door closed she heard a loud, "Mary Jane!"

A few seconds after she was at her desk the phone rang. "Strange gift, Mary Jane," said Bill with the hint of a smile in his voice. She told him what she had done on Saturday. "Stay with it, Mary Jane. I don't know what a fish market has to do with First Guarantee, but if you can make me smile with the day I have ahead, you may be on to something."

When she hung up the phone, she was aware that her relationship with Bill was somehow different. *I don't think many on his staff stand up to him*, she thought. *Strange as it seems, I believe he appreciates the fact that I have chosen not to be intimidated.*

The Field Trip

At the first of her two Monday morning staff meetings she got right to the point. "I'm impressed and heartened by how you have worked at finding ways to remind us all that we can choose our attitude each day. The Choose Your Attitude Menu was a great idea, and it's the talk of the building. It's fun at last to hear some positive comments. Now it's time to take the next step. There is something I want you all to experience, so we are going on a lunchtime field trip. This group will go on Wednesday, the other group on Thursday. Brown bag lunches will be provided, so just bring yourselves.

"The field trip will be to a place many of you have visited before. We are going to a special fish market where we will study energy in action. There are a bunch of guys there who have solved their version of our problem. It will be our task to see if we can understand and apply their secrets for success."

"I have a dental appointment." "I have plans for lunch that day." The voices of those around her rose with objections. She was surprised when she heard a strong voice, her own, say, "I expect you all to be there and to rearrange your plans to make that possible. This is important."

On Wednesday, the first group met in the lobby and headed for the market. "All I want you to do is observe the scene you are about to see." She chuckled, "Be sure to keep your yogurt handy." Her use of the Yogi Berra quote, "You can observe a lot by watching," received one polite laugh. *Well, it's a start*, she thought.

The fish market was busy when they arrived, and they quickly dispersed. That made it hard for her to watch reactions, but she did notice a few of her staff obviously enjoying themselves. She saw John and Steve in close conversation with one of the fish guys and moved closer to observe. "When you are present with people you look right at them . . . just like being with your best friend . . . everything is going on around you but you're still taking care of just them," said the red-headed fish guy to John.

Good for John and Steve, she thought. *Great initiative.*

On Thursday the second group made the trip, most likely briefed by the first group. There were almost no questions, and the group was rather reserved until something special happened. Stephanie, a long-time employee, was asked if she wanted to go behind the counter and catch a fish. Although she had seemed quite shy at work, she accepted. Two fish slipped through her grasp, much to the delight of the crowd and the special amusement of her coworkers. On the third try, she made a dazzling bare-handed catch which was followed by thunderous applause, catcalls, and whistles. She was hooked as the fish guys made her day.

Stephanie seemed to open the door for others. As the fish flew overhead, the gang from First Guarantee did a lot more than raise their yogurt cups in the air.

Friday Afternoon Meetings

On Friday afternoon, she met with each group separately. "Wouldn't it be neat to work in a place where you could have as much fun as the guys do at the Pike Place Fish market?" she asked. There were a few nods and some smiles as the image of a flying fish passed through their minds. Stephanie had the biggest smile of all. Then reality set in.

In both groups, protest followed the initial smiles. "We don't sell fish!" Mark said. "We don't have anything to throw," added Beth. "It's a guy thing," contributed Ann. "Our work is boring," said another. One wisecracker said, "Let's throw the purchase orders."

"You're right; this isn't a fish market; what we do is different. What I'm asking is: Are you interested in having a place to work which has as much energy as the world famous Pike Place Fish market? A place where you smile more often. A place where you have positive feelings about what you do and the way you do it. A place you look forward to being at each day. You've already demonstrated that in many ways we can choose our attitude. Are you interested in taking it further?"

Stephanie spoke up. "I like the people here; they're good people. But I hate coming to work. I can hardly breathe in this place. It's like a morgue. So I might as well admit it: I've been looking for another job. If we could find a way to create some life here, it would be a more satisfying place to work, and I would definitely consider staying."

"Thank you for your honesty and courage, Stephanie."

Steve added, "I want to make this place more fun."

Randy raised his hand.

"Yes, Randy?"

"You talked about your personal situation the other day, Mary Jane. I never heard a boss do that before and it got me thinking. I'm raising my son alone, and I need this job and the benefits that go with it. I don't like to make waves, but I'm sorry to admit I sometimes take out my frustrations on people in other departments. They seem to have it so good, while I'm trapped here in this pit. You've helped me realize that we make this place a pit by the way we act here. Well, if we can choose to make it a pit, then we can also choose something else. The thought of doing that has me really excited. If I can learn to have fun and be happy here, well, then I guess I can also learn to do that in other parts of my life."

"Thanks, Randy." She turned and looked directly at him with gratitude, adding, "I see a few heads nodding, and I know you've said something really important here today. You have touched me and others with your words from the heart. Thanks. Thank you for your contribution. Let's build a better workplace, a place we love to be in.

"On Monday we'll start the process of putting the Fish Philosophy to work on the third floor. Between now and then, I want you to think about your personal experience at the fish market and write down any questions or ideas you have. When we get together next time, we can discuss how to proceed. Just let what you saw at the market stimulate your thinking."

The wisecracker popped up again, "Well, if we can't throw the purchase orders paper, can't we at least throw the confetti from the shredder?" Laughter filled the room. *That feels good*, she thought.

Mary Jane then passed copies of an outline she had developed at the market and walked everyone through her personal observations. She encouraged her staff to remember and record their own thoughts over the weekend.

After the second meeting ended, Mary Jane retreated to her office and sat exhausted at her desk. *I gave them something to think about over the weekend. But will they?* Little did she know that half a dozen of her employees would find a reason to visit the market again that weekend, many of them with family and friends.

MARY JANE'S OUTLINE

Choose Your Attitude—The fish guys are aware that they choose their attitude each day. One of the fish guys said, "When you are doing what you are doing, who are you being? Are you being impatient and bored, or are you being *world famous*? You are going to act differently if you are being world famous." Who do we want to be while we do our work?

Play—The fish guys have fun while they work, and fun is energizing. How could we have more fun and create more energy?

Make Their Day—The fish guys include the customers in their good time. They engage their customers in ways which create energy and goodwill. Who are our customers and how can we engage them in a way that will make their day? How could we make each other's days?

Be Present—The fish guys are fully present at work. What can they teach us about being present for each other and our customers?

**Please bring your thoughts
with you on Monday.**

MJR

That Weekend at the Fish Market

"Teacher give you an assignment?"

Stephanie looked up and simultaneously saw a fish fly through the air and Lonnie's smiling face. "Hi. I guess you might say my boss gave me some homework."

"That wouldn't be Mary Jane, would it?"

"How did you know?" Her response was drowned out by a monger shouting, "Three tuna flying away to Paris," with a fake French accent. Lonnie seemed to hear her anyway. *No wonder they're so good at being present*, she thought. *They have to be if they want to hear anything above all this commotion.*

"I saw you here during the week with Mary Jane's group. You are also the first yogurt dude I remember catching a fish as long as I've been here."

"Really?"

"So how can I help you? You seem puzzled."

She looked down at her notes. "I think I understand *be present*, the way you are right now with me. And when I was catching the fish—well . . . I will never forget the way you made my day. Play is something that comes easy for me—I love to enjoy myself

79

and fool around. But *choose your attitude* is still a bit of a mystery. I mean, doesn't your attitude have a lot to do with the way you are treated and what happens to you?"

"I know just the person you need to ask about attitude: Wolf. Wolf was on his way to a career as a professional race car driver when he had a serious accident. Well, I'll let Wolf tell the story. We need to go back into the locker. Will you be warm enough?"

"Can we come, too?"

Stephanie looked to her left and saw Steve, Randy, and one very cute child. After introductions, they all went back to talk to Wolf, who told them how, while he was recovering from his accident, he learned to choose his attitude every day. His words made a deep impression on the three and they vowed to share them with their fellow workers at the Monday meeting.

Afterward, Steve had to take off, but Stephanie, Randy, and Randy's son went across the street to a café. The adults sipped coffee, while Randy's son ate a giant chocolate chip muffin.

"You know," said Stephanie, "we might as well clean up our toxic energy dump because there is no guarantee the next job will be any different. And think about it. How many bosses are there like Mary Jane? I really respect her. Think about what she's been through. I hear she even stood up to that jerk Bill Walsh. None of the other department managers ever stood up to that bully. I mean that counts for something, doesn't it, Randy?"

"Stephanie, you're reading my mind. If these fish guys could do what they have done, the sky is the limit for us with a boss like Mary Jane. It isn't going to be easy. Some of our coworkers are as frightened as I used to be. They're skeptical because they're scared. Perhaps if we provide a positive example it will help. All I know is that things won't get better until we choose to make them better—and I want things to get better."

As Stephanie walked to her car she noticed Betty and her husband. She waved and then became aware of three other people from her office in the crowd. *Great!* she thought.

The Plan Unfolds

There was a buzz in the room as the first group assembled for the Monday morning meeting. Mary Jane opened the meeting by saying, "We're here to clean up what has been called a toxic energy dump. Today we'll see if we have any additional lessons from the market and then decide on our next steps. Did anyone think of anything during the weekend that we should consider before moving on?"

Stephanie and Randy jumped to their feet and took turns recalling their conversation with Wolf. Stephanie began.

"Wolf was really cool, although he was a little scary at first. I mean his voice is like a growl. Anyway, he told us his story of having a career as a professional race car driver torn away from him by a freak accident. He said he wallowed in pity for a while and then, when his girlfriend left him and friends stopped calling, he realized he had a basic choice to make. He could choose to live and to live fully, or he could let life slip away in a series of missed opportunities. He has been making the choice to live fully every day since. It was quite a story."

"My son was fascinated with Wolf," continued Randy. "Wolf really got me thinking about our situation here on three, and how much power we have over the kind of place we create. We could make three into a great place to work if we learn the lesson of Wolf. We must choose our attitude every day and choose it well."

Steve also offered some observations.

"Thanks, Steve. Thank you, Randy. Thanks, Stephanie. It sounds like you were busy this weekend. And thanks for not asking for overtime!" After the laughter died down, Mary Jane asked, "Who else has something to offer which will help us understand these points?" Forty-five minutes later, Mary Jane decided to bring the discussion to a close. "Any ideas on where we go from here?"

"Why don't we form a team for each of the four ingredients?" said one of the newer employees.

There were a number of nods.

"All right," said Mary Jane. "Let me make sure the other half agrees with this approach. Why don't you sign up for the group you prefer; if the other group goes along, I will put everything in memo form and get it to you tomorrow. Is there anything else to discuss?"

At the end of the meeting she passed around a sign-up sheet and asked each of them to sign up for one of the four teams. The second group fully supported the idea of teams and seemed relieved to have a concrete plan of action.

The Teams Go to Work

The Play Team had a few too many volunteers, so Mary Jane did a little gentle negotiating. "I have a genuine Pike Place Fish market T-shirt for the first three volunteers who will move from Play to Choose Your Attitude or Be Present." Once the teams were balanced, she put together a memo with the general guidelines and expectations.

TEAM GUIDELINES

- Teams will have six weeks to meet, study their topic, collect additional information, and put together a presentation that will be made to the group as a whole at an off-site meeting.

- Each presentation must have some action items that we can consider for implementation.

- Teams will be responsible for setting their own meeting times and may use two hours of work

---

time each week for team business. Arrangements must be made to cover the work of those at team meetings during business hours.

- Each team has a budget of $200 to be spent at its discretion.

- Teams will facilitate their own meetings.

- I will be available to troubleshoot if the team reaches an impasse, but I would rather the team work out its issues as a team.

**Good luck! Let's create a place
where we all want to work!**

MJR

Team Reports

Six weeks had passed since the teams started meeting. The presentations would be made today. Mary Jane had asked Bill if people from other departments could handle essential functions for a morning, so the whole group could meet; Bill surprised her by offering to help personally as well as organize the coverage. "I don't know what you're doing," he said, "but I already sense a new level of energy on three. Keep up the good work and let me know if there is anything else I can do."

She was a bit nervous. Each of the teams had asked her to meet with them at least once, and she had done her best to be helpful and supportive without taking control. Although she had been asked for reading material and the use of a conference room in the last two weeks, none of the teams had requested more than that. She really didn't have a clue about the specifics of any of the four presentations. And today was the day they would go off-site to hear the team reports.

At nine in the morning, they all walked down to the Alexis Hotel as Bill and the other volunteers arrived to cover the office. "Good luck," he said.

They arrived at the Alexis and were directed to the Market Room. *Appropriate*, she thought. She had decided that the Choose Your Attitude Team should present last. She had explained to each team: "I want the ingredient that underlies all of the others to be the last thing we consider."

She felt a surge of emotion as she entered the meeting room. The room was a sea of color, music, and energy. Balloons were attached to each chair, and colorful flower arrangements brought the room to life. *They have responded to the challenge*, she thought. *Their clocks are wound up again.* The biggest surprise of the day was sitting in the back of the room in his full fishmonger outfit. It was Lonnie. She took the seat next to him as things began.

The Play Team

One of the members of the Play Team called the room to attention and asked the whole staff to come up front. As directions were given, everyone stood around rather awkwardly. "Our report is in the form of a game which we'll all play," said Betty, the Play Team spokesperson.

The Play Team had designed a game using a path of circles cut from colored paper and arranged on the floor so you could step from one circle to the next as the music played. Each circle had written on it a key point from their report. When the music stopped, the person standing on a specific circle was asked to read the text on it. It was sort of like a cakewalk. There were two groups of items. One was a list of benefits and the other a list of implementation ideas. *Great work*, thought Mary Jane.

Benefits of Play

- Happy people treat others well.

- Fun leads to creativity.

- The time passes quickly.

- Having a good time is healthy.

- Work becomes a reward and not just a way to rewards.

Implementing Play on the Third Floor

- Post signs saying, THIS IS A PLAYGROUND. WATCH OUT FOR ADULT CHILDREN.

- Start a joke-of-the-month contest with its own bulletin board.

- Add more color and make the environment more interesting.

- Add more life with plants and an aquarium.

- Special events such as a lunchtime comedian.

- Small lights to turn on when it is time to lighten up a bit or when you have a good idea.

- Instruction in creativity.

- A designated creativity area called the Sand Box.

- Form an ongoing play committee to keep the ideas flowing.

The Make Their Day Team

The Make Their Day Team was next. "Go out into the hall and have some coffee while we set up," was their first instruction. When everyone was called back into the room, the staff was divided into small groups with a member of the Make Their Day Team in each group. Stephanie described the assignment as everyone milled around.

"I want each group to take fifteen minutes to develop a list of strategies for supporting and enhancing the work of a key group of people, our internal customers. But first I want to introduce some data. These are the findings of a customer survey we performed.

Take a deep breath because you aren't going to like what you see." A slide went up. A wave of shock passed through the room; there was actually one audible gasp.

RESULTS OF CUSTOMER SURVEY

1. Our customers dread working with us. They call us "the sleepwalkers" because we seem positively sedated to them. They would prefer a good fight than the impersonal treatment they receive.

2. The work we do is adequate, but we rarely offer to extend ourselves in order to help them serve the external customer. We do our job, period, and no more.

3. We often treat our customers as if they are interrupting us.

4. We frequently pass our customers around from one person to another without ever conveying an interest in solving the problem. We appear to be attempting to avoid responsibility.

5. Our customers joke about our response, or lack thereof, to a problem which arises after 4. They laugh about the stampede to the elevator at 4:30.

6. Our customers question our very commitment to the enterprise.

7. We are referred to as the "last stage of decline."

8. Discussions have started concerning the possibility of replacing our department with an outside contractor.

Stephanie said, "Our team was first shocked and then angered by these findings. Slowly we came to realize that the customers feel how they feel. No matter what excuses we offer or what kind of spin we put on it, it doesn't change how our internal customers feel. That's the reality as they see it. The question is, what are we going to do about it?"

Another team member continued with considerable passion, "I don't think we realize how important our role is in the business of First Guarantee. Many people count on us, and they look bad when we drop the ball or drag our feet. The fact that many of us have other obligations and that we aren't very high on the compensation scale is not their problem. They're just trying to serve the customers who pay our salaries—and we're seen by them as an impediment to high quality service."

Then Stephanie said, "We need your ideas and need them badly. Please help us to take a step away from the dump and toward making our customers' day. Each group has forty-five minutes to come up with as many ideas as possible. Please find a seat and get started. The member of our team will serve as scribe." There was silence for a while. Then the groups began attacking the problem, still riding on the energy generated by the first presentation.

When the time had come, Stephanie announced, "Let's take a short break while the scribes integrate their notes." After ten minutes, she reconvened the staff. "Here's a quick look at the results," she said, "and this award goes to the members of the table four group." The people from table four came up to receive their Make Their Day buttons. Smaller buttons were passed out to everyone else. Attention turned to their summary report.

Benefits of Make Their Day

- It is good for business.

- Serving our customers well will give us the satisfaction that comes to those who serve others. It will focus our attention, away from our problems onto how we can make a positive difference to others. This is healthy, will feel good, and will unleash even more energy.

Implementing Make Their Day

- Stagger our hours so there is coverage from 7 A.M. until 6 P.M. This will be good for our customers (and may also be helpful to some of us who need different start times).

- Pull together some focus groups to study ways we can be of service to our customers. Should we have specialty groups, for instance, focusing on specific customer categories?

- Have a monthly and an annual award for service, based on the recommendation of our customers who said their day had been made.

- Implement a 360-degree feedback process which includes our customers.

- Appoint a special task force dedicated to surprising and delighting our customers.

- Ask our key customers to "come out and play" once a month.

- Study what it would take to implement the "moment of truth" idea, which started at SAS, Scandanavian Airlines. We would try to make every transaction with our customers a positive transaction.

Mary Jane quietly rejoiced. "If they care this much, we can turn our department around. Stephanie is on fire and her group shows signs of catching the same enthusiasm. We can do it! I know we can!" Out of the corner of her eye she noticed that Lonnie had a pleased look on his face.

The Present Moment Team

The Present Moment Team took an entirely different approach, which gave a welcome change of pace. With soothing music playing in the background, one of the group members said, "Close your eyes and relax for a minute. Breathe deeply as I guide you through a number of visualizations that will help us be fully present."

When she was finished, she said, "Now listen as members of our group offer some thoughts. Stay relaxed, try to even your breathing, and keep your eyes closed."

A number of inspirational readings followed. One of the readings went something like this:

> *The past is history*
> *The future is a mystery*
> *Today is a gift*
> *That is why we call it the present*

John offered a personal story. "I was living a busy life," he said with sadness in his voice, "trying to make ends meet and working both sides against the middle. One day my daughter asked me to go to the park. I told her it was a wonderful idea, but I had a lot to do at that moment. I said she should wait until later, after I had a chance to catch up. But there always seemed to be some urgent and pressing work to do and the days passed. Days led to weeks and weeks to months." With a choking voice, he said that four years passed and he never did go to the park. His daughter is now fifteen and no longer interested in the park, nor, for that matter, in him.

John paused and took a deep breath. "I talked to one of the fish guys about being present, and I realized how infrequently I was really present at home or at work. The fish guy invited me to visit the market with the whole family. My daughter didn't want to go, but I finally wore her down and she came along. We had a good time, and I worked on being present with my children. When my wife took my son down the street to the toy store, I sat down with my daughter and told her how sorry I was that I really hadn't been there for her. I told her I hoped she could forgive me and that while I couldn't change the past, I let her know that I was now dedicated to being present in the present. She said I wasn't that bad a dad—I just needed to lighten up a little. I've got a ways to go," he said, "but I'm improving. Being present could help me recover something I wasn't aware I had lost: a relationship with my daughter."

After John was finished, Lonnie whispered to Mary Jane, "The fish guy was Jacob. He has been higher than a kite ever since. He's a new guy, and it was his first taste of really helping someone."

Janet also became quite emotional when she described a coworker at her previous job. "This person kept trying to get my attention," she said, "but I was distracted by personal issues, and we never connected. Then all hell broke loose. It seems she was way over her head and was covering up the lack of progress by issuing imaginary reports. By the time it all came to light, it was too late to correct. She lost her job, the company lost a client and a great deal of money, and I eventually lost my job because we were unable to replace the work. All of this could have been avoided if I had been present for a coworker who was reaching out for help."

Then Beth told a personal story of riding on a stationary bike in front of the TV while trying to catch up on some reading, when her son came in and sat down on the couch. She could tell he was distressed. "A mother knows these things," she said. "In the past I would have continued doing what I was doing while talking to him. But experience and a divorce have taught me that efficiency isn't always wise or nice with loved ones. So I turned off the TV, got off of the bicycle, set the magazines aside, and spent the next hour listening deeply as my son described the difficult time he was having just coping with life. I was really glad I made the choice to be fully present."

A few more members of the group told a mix of personal and business stories. Then they confirmed their commitment to being present for one another and for internal customers. "When you are present you show consideration for the other person," one of the team members added. They also committed to being fully present when discussing an issue, whether with each other or a customer; they would truly listen and not allow themselves to be distracted. They encouraged one another to ask, "Is this a good time? Are you present?" To support one another in asking these questions they established a code phrase. "You seem distracted," was chosen as a special code to signal a possible present moment issue. Everyone agreed to give it a try. And everyone also agreed never again to read or answer e-mails while talking on the phone with a colleague or customer.

The Choose Your Attitude Team

Last came the Choose Your Attitude Team. Their verbal report was brief and to the point. "Here are the benefits our team identified as a result of choosing your attitude.

"First, by accepting that you choose your attitude, you demonstrate a level of personal accountability and proactivity which will fill the third floor with energy, all by itself.

"Second, choosing your attitude and acting like a victim are mutually exclusive.

"Third, we hope the attitude you choose is to bring your best self to work and to love the work you do. We may not be able to do exactly what we love at the present time, but any of us can choose to love what we do. We can bring our best qualities to our work—it is our choice. If we can accomplish this one thing, our work area will become an oasis of energy, flexibility, and creativity in a tough industry."

Implementing Choose Your Attitude

Margaret, the highly animated team spokesperson, suggested that the implementation plan for Choose Your Attitude was a highly personal one. "Many of us have lost sight of our ability to choose. We must be compassionate with each other but work together to nurture our ability to exercise free will. If you don't know you have choices or don't believe you have choices, you don't. There are people in our group who have had some very difficult life experiences. It will take some of us quite a while to be able to internalize this idea that we can choose our attitude."

Another team member continued, "We have identified two ways to implement Choose Your Attitude and have already taken some steps.

"First, we've purchased for everyone copies of a little book titled *Personal Accountability: The Path to a Rewarding Work Life*. Our group will organize discussion groups after you have had a chance to read it. If that goes well, we will follow with discussions of *Raving Fans*, *The Seven Habits of Highly Effective People*, *Gung Ho!*, and *The Road Less Traveled*. All of these books can help us understand the concept of choosing an attitude.

"Second, we've prepared an attitude menu for everyone to use back at the office. You've seen a version of this before. We still don't know who put the first one on our office door, so we can't give credit. Now you have your personal menu for each day."

Mary Jane looked down at her attitude menu. It had two sides. On one side was a frowning face surrounded by words like *angry*, *disinterested*, and *bitter*. On the other side was a smiling face with words like *energetic*, *caring*, *vital*, *supportive*, and *creative*. At the top it said: THE CHOICE IS YOURS. It was a nice extension of the menu over the main door to the third floor. Mary Jane jumped up and set off to congratulate each and every member of her staff with Lonnie a few steps behind her, providing his own brand of encouragement. It was after lunch before she finished talking with everyone. She now knew they were well on their way to cleaning up the toxic energy dump.

Lonnie walked Mary Jane back to First Guarantee. It wasn't surprising that they attracted a few stares: a businesswoman and a fishmonger in full regalia. What was surprising was how many knew Lonnie.

"So, your boss doesn't know about the job offer, does he," said Lonnie. Two weeks earlier, Mary Jane had received an unexpected call from First Guarantee's main competitor, making an attempt to lure her away.

"I don't think so. I believe the recruiter talked to my old boss. The woman who recently left First Guarantee for a wonderful position in Portland. I haven't said anything at work."

"I couldn't understand your turning down such a lucrative offer, but now I see why. You are committed to this process, and you couldn't let these people down, could you?"

"That was part of it, Lonnie. But after working so hard to make First Guarantee more fun and a better place to work, why would I leave? The good times are just starting."

🐟Sunday, February 7: The Coffee Shop One Year Later

Mary Jane opened her book, *Simple Abundance*, and turned to February 7.

This stuff is timeless, she thought. *A year ago I was sitting here, wondering how I would ever clean up the toxic energy dump. In fact, it was here that I realized I was part of the problem and needed to lead myself before I could lead the group.*

Those committee reports at the hotel were a great start. The staff had always been capable of much more—it just took some fish guys to bring those capabilities to light. The third floor is a different place now, and our new problem is all the people from around the company who want to work there. I guess the energy was there all the time.

And the Chairwoman's Award was such a nice surprise. I think the chairwoman was caught off guard when I asked for so many copies of the award. One for me, one for Bill, one for each employee in the department, and one for Lonnie and each of the other fish guys. I enjoy seeing it hanging above their cash register at the world famous Pike Place Fish market and displayed prominently in Lonnie's living room.

She opened her journal to one of her favorite selections she had transcribed, a piece written by John Gardner on the meaning in life.

Meaning

Meaning is not something you stumble across, like the answer to a riddle or the prize in a treasure hunt. Meaning is something you build into your life. You build it out of your own past, out of your affections and loyalties, out of the experience of humankind as it is passed on to you, out of your own talent and

FISH!

*understanding, out of the things you believe in, out of the
things and people you love, out of the values for which you
are willing to sacrifice something. The ingredients are
there. You are the only one who can put them together
into that pattern that will be your life. Let it be a life that
has dignity and meaning for you. If it does, then the
particular balance of success or failure is of less account.*

John Gardner

Mary Jane was wiping tears from her eyes as she closed the journal where she kept her thoughts and inspirational "keepers."

"Lonnie, could I have a piece of that scone, before you finish the whole darn thing?" Lonnie had been sitting quietly across from her, reading. He pushed the plate over to her. When she reached down for the scone, she found instead a small diamond engagement ring sitting in the large open mouth of a fish head. She looked up at Lonnie, who had a large question mark on his nervous face. Choking with laughter, she sputtered, "Oh, Lonnie! Yes! Yes I will! But don't you ever stop playing?"

It had been a cold, dark, dreary day in Seattle on the outside. But something far different had been chosen for the inside.

THE CHAIRWOMAN'S
AWARD CEREMONY

The chairwoman came to the podium and looked out at the audience. She glanced down at her notes and then looked up again saying, "I can't remember a prouder moment in my life than tonight. Something very special has happened at First Guarantee. In a back room operation on the third floor, Mary Jane Ramirez and her team members rediscovered that satisfying, rewarding work can be a choice we make when we come through the door in the morning. It is as simple as asking, 'Is this going to be a good day?' And answering, 'Yes! I choose to make this a great day!'

"Long-term employees have the enthusiasm of new hires and what was thought to be routine work has been transformed into value-added activity. I understand the ingredients for this transformation were discovered at a local fish market. The team on the third floor observed that if you could make a fish market a great place to work, you could choose to make any department of First Guarantee a great place to work.

"The ingredients of this transformation are inscribed on a plaque which has been hung in the front entrance of our headquarters building. It reads as follows:

OUR WORKPLACE

As you enter this place of work please *choose* to make today a great day. Your colleagues, customers, team members, and you yourself will be thankful. Find ways to *play*. We can be serious about our work without being serious about ourselves. Stay focused in order to *be present* when your customers and team members most need you. And should you feel your energy lapsing, try this surefire remedy: Find someone who needs a helping hand, a word of support, or a good ear—and *make their day*.

FiSH!™
TALES

CONTENTS

CONTENTS

INTRODUCTION

Over the last few years the story of a remarkable group of fishmongers from the Pike Place Fish market in Seattle has stimulated many of us to consider new possibilities for our work and our lives. As the poet David Whyte put it, we are finding ways to "make work a reward and not just a way to rewards." We are also finding ways to live our time on this planet full to the brim as a testament to the preciousness of life.

The story of these unusual fish guys was told in the book *FISH!* In it we described four principles that help foster a great life at work—"Play," "Make Their Day," "Be There," and "Choose Your Attitude." These principles are a part of what we call the FISH! Philosophy. Living this philosophy results in a workplace where the quality of life is satisfying and meaningful, and the experience for customers, internal and external, is compelling.

The core message of the book you are now holding, *FISH! TALES*, is that a richer and more rewarding life may simply be a few choices away from where you are right now. Each of the first four sections in this book features a real-life story that highlights one of the four FISH! principles. Still, the other principles also are depicted in each feature story. It must be this way. Play, for example, operates in a context of being there, making someone's day, and choosing your attitude. It is the context that keeps play appropriate.

After each main story are several short stories—we call

them "small bites"—to further illustrate the main principle. Feel free to sample these at random.

If your spirit is inspired by the real-life stories in this book, we hope your actions will be guided by the 12 weeks of transformational activities at the end of *FISH! TALES*.

Throughout this book, Steve Lundin will be your guide and narrator. You will hear his voice and perspective, in first person, as he tells the story of FISH!, introduces the four feature stories, and takes you through the 12 weeks of activities.

The rest of us join in at various other times. Phil Strand wrote the feature stories. John Christensen and Harry Paul contributed their considerable experience working with the FISH! Philosophy and shared their insights.

Now, let's go fishing!

The Fundamentals of FISH!

John Christensen and I, each in our own way, have been curious about what is possible at work. I worked at a camp for children with serious physical challenges for six summers. After banging around the "real" world for many years I came to realize that Camp Courage was one of the most joyous workplaces I had ever experienced. I began to wonder why organizations full of able-bodied people were often so joyless.

John brought a social-service background and an artist's eye to the world of work. He was intensely curious about the occasional workplace he encountered that exuded an abundance of energy and passion. He would come back to the office with a story of a shoemaker who was passionate about his work or a furniture company with a spirit that soared. We found we were both searching for an image that would help inspire all of us to see what was possible at work, knowing we all are destined to spend a majority of our lives there.

In 1997, John and I flew to Seattle and hauled our film gear to the quaint little town of Langley on Whidbey Island. There we filmed the poet David Whyte, who is known for

1

the message he shares with organizations about bringing one's whole self to work. We became immersed in conversations about wholeheartedness in the workplace. David quoted a friend of his who said, "The antidote to exhaustion is not necessarily rest. The antidote to exhaustion is wholeheartedness. It is those things you do halfheartedly that really wear you out."

Later, talking to the camera, David recalled an answer he gave on a radio interview when asked what it was like to take his message into organizations. He responded, "Sometimes it is quite marvelous and sometimes it is like visiting the prison population." When he said this I was surprised and shocked. Then he continued, "I don't mean organizations or businesses are necessarily prisons, but sometimes we make prisons of them by the way we live there."

Our time with David was a feast for the soul. We left Whidbey Island with a greater understanding about this as-yet theoretical workplace image we sought.

We drove back to Seattle and spent Friday night there. I was flying out the next morning, but John was staying until the following night. We asked the concierge to suggest places a guy from Minnesota might visit on Saturday. She recommended the Pike Place Market. We knew little about Seattle and this seemed like a fine idea, since John loves to shop.

John was on one end of the market when he heard laughing and screaming. Like a child following the Pied Piper, he was drawn to the sound, and found himself in the back of an enthusiastic crowd. Suddenly the crowd parted and he came face-to-face with the source of the commotion. It was the World Famous Pike Place Fish market.

If you've ever been to Pike Place Fish, you know that when a customer places an order, the fishmongers standing in front of the counter throw the fish over the counter to coworkers for wrapping. They make some spectacular catches and the crowd loves it. The fishmongers regularly invite delighted customers behind the counter to try their luck at catching.

But on this day, as John stood in the middle of a cheering crowd, he was more interested in the way the fishmongers threw themselves into their work. The market was crowded and noisy, but when one of the fishmongers focused on a customer, it was like they were the only two people in the place. Everywhere John looked, both employees and customers were smiling, laughing, and most important, connecting with each other. Not coincidentally, the cash registers were ringing like crazy.

John watched in fascination for almost an hour. Suddenly a fishmonger broke his trance. "Hi!" he said. "My name's Shawn." His hair was red, his smile was huge, and his eyes twinkled mischievously.

"What's going on here?" John asked.

Shawn answered with a question of his own. "Did you eat lunch today?"

"Yeah," John said, wondering what he was getting at.

"How was the service?" Shawn asked.

John shrugged his shoulders. "Okay, I guess."

"But did the waiter really connect with you?"

Connect with me? What in the heck is he talking about? John thought to himself.

Shawn's eyes locked on John's. "See, this is our moment together, yours and mine, and I want it to be like you and I are best friends."

John started to understand what was happening here. A bunch of fishmongers—not MBA professors or organizational gurus—were showing him how to bring more fun, passion, focus, and commitment to work.

As John continued to watch the fishmongers engage and connect with customers, a drama off to the side caught his attention. One of the fish guys had attached a crayfish to a young boy's pants. The boy was startled and began crying. The fishmonger got down on his knees and crawled over to the boy, who was clinging tightly to his mother, and asked first for forgiveness and then for a hug. The fish guy had misjudged this child, but his recovery spoke volumes.

John's mind drifted back to the previous week, when he had taken his daughter, who has severe asthma, to the doctor because she was having trouble breathing. As they stood in front of the registration desk, Kelsey gasping for each breath, a cold voice asked them a number of questions. Its owner typed the responses, never looking up, and then barked, "Take a seat."

Finally a disembodied voice from the hall shouted, "Kelsey Christensen." The nurse, barely looking at Kelsey, carelessly whacked the top of her head with the measuring device attached to the scale. The nurse marched down the hall as John and Kelsey struggled to catch up, then stopped by a door and pointed inside, never looking back.

John looked at the boy at the fish market, who was now smiling and holding the crayfish. *Why would a fishmonger give more care to a frightened child than the professionals in the health-care clinic where I took Kelsey?* he wondered.

John watched one fishmonger after another engage customers with all the attentiveness of the best caregiver. He knew he had to capture this image on film. His intuition told him it would be hard to watch these guys at work, see the power of the way they live each day, and not be inspired. He suddenly felt anxious. What if they said no? Two hours later he had finally gotten to the point where he was ready to broach the subject with the owner. He said he was a filmmaker and before he could continue, one of the guys said, "Where have you been? We have been waiting for you."

ChartHouse Learning soon brought its cameras to Pike Place Fish. After watching hours of footage, we saw that the fishmongers created their engaging environment through a few fundamentals—simple but powerful choices that we all can make. We translated these actions into a new language we call the FISH! Philosophy. We explored four of the principles in a documentary-style video called *FISH!* They include:

PLAY— *Work made fun gets done, especially when we choose to do serious tasks in a lighthearted, spontaneous way. Play is not just an activity; it's a state of mind that brings new energy to the tasks at hand and sparks creative solutions.*

FiSH! TALES

MAKE THEIR DAY– *When you "make someone's day" (or moment) through a small kindness or unforgettable engagement, you can turn even routine encounters into special memories.*

BE THERE– *The glue in our humanity is in being fully present for one another. Being there also is a great way to practice wholeheartedness and fight burnout, for it is those halfhearted tasks you perform while juggling other things that wear you out.*

CHOOSE YOUR ATTITUDE– *When you look for the worst you will find it everywhere. When you learn you have the power to choose your response to what life brings, you can look for the best and find opportunities you never imagined possible. If you find yourself with an attitude that is not what you want it to be, you can choose a new one.*

A year after the *FISH!* video came out, we explored these principles further in a book we also called *FISH!* (Pretty tricky, huh?) We invented a story about a workplace where people were so disconnected from their work that their department was known as the "Toxic Energy Dump." The book illustrated how the lessons of the fish market could apply to typical organizational challenges.

Over the next few years, through the film and the book, the FISH! Philosophy spread into organizations around the world. People began to reinvent what their time at work could be about, and the passion, energy, and accountability they discovered led to surprising business improvements. They shared their inspiring stories with us and, through their experiences, our understanding of what is possible through these principles expanded and deepened. You will find some of these stories in this book.

The people in these stories are no different from you or me. What makes them extraordinary is that one day they each made the choice to try to live more joyfully, responsibly, and wholeheartedly. The next day they chose again. And the day after that and the day after that . . .

Section One-PLAY

Play is not just an activity; it's a state of mind that brings new energy and sparks creativity.

Remember this old warning? "Boys and girls, playtime is over, get back to work." Most of us learned early in life that work and play are separate, and that if you are playing you could not possibly be working. But to have a livable work environment, one in which human beings thrive, a certain amount of playfulness or lightheartedness is required. We have found no exception to this rule. The alternative is what Ken Blanchard refers to as an "epidemic of tight underwear." Not a pleasant image.

An innovative environment demands even more play. Habitually following the direct "all business" line from Point A to Point B may *seem* more efficient, but it constricts one's capacity to generate new solutions when needed. The freedom to be playful—to take a winding, curious line—expands creative opportunities (as well as the minds and spirits of the humans involved). The spirit that allows people to wear a goofy tie or to laugh out loud without fearing what others think is the same spirit that encourages them to consider new ideas which expand the boundaries of what they used to think was possible. Creativity becomes an adult game of make-believe ("Hey, what if . . . ?") we can all play.

The fishmongers know that play can stimulate creativity. When a customer placed an order, they used to walk from behind the counter to pick up the fish, then had to hike all the way back around to wrap the fish and ring up the purchase. But one day they did something different. One of the fish guys threw a salmon over the counter to another. Eureka! Not only did they create a new kind of performance art, but they became more productive by eliminating a lot of walking back and forth.

Despite the benefits of a lighthearted workplace, it's amazing how much fear the thought of play strikes into the heart of management. When an executive for a large fast-food chain said, "You want us to tell 300,000 teenagers they can play?" he probably imagined the world's largest food fight.

One reason for the fear may be that we aren't sure what play is. The same people who are drawn to the playfulness of Pike Place Fish often can't imagine how they could ever replicate such an atmosphere in their own workplace. "What can *we* throw at work?" they ask.

The fishmongers have the answer. "There are a million different ways of playing," they say. "It doesn't have to be throwing a fish!"

Actuaries, teachers, or engineers will find different ways to be playful than the fish guys. That is the point. Play is not restricted to a toy or a game. It is the lighthearted feeling you release inside people when they are enthused, committed, and free of fear. A successful budget meeting in which serious work is being done can stimulate the same feeling as a picnic.

SEND ME YOUR IMPLEMENTATION MANUAL FOR PLAY

Three weeks prior to a sales meeting at which we were to introduce the FISH! Philosophy, we received an unusual request: "We have all 57 branches coming to this meeting and we want our people to be more playful at work, but could you send your objectives for play? Or maybe you could send an implementation manual to show us how to play."

At first I thought he was joking. Can you imagine telling your children to go out to play, and having them say, "Great! What are the objectives?" But that didn't matter to the caller. He wanted nothing less than predetermined outcomes from this "play thing."

How could I help him understand? "What about some bullet points?" I suggested.

"Anything to help explain the play thing."

So I sent a whole flip-chart sheet full of bullet points. No words, just bullet points. Suddenly he got it! Play can't be implemented or rolled out to all 57 branches like a new accounting system. (My colleague Carr Hagerman makes this point well. Preparing to juggle knives or tools, he says, "You can play with an implement, but you can't implement play.")

Play must come from within and so you can only *invite* play.

We need to create our objectives together as a team. By the way, the meeting went great—and those concerned about the "play thing" were the most receptive to a playful atmosphere.

Play also requires trust. You can try to duplicate what the fishmongers do on the surface, but if you don't have the shared commitment and trust that make playfulness possible at work, it may not happen.

A hospital wanted to invite more playfulness into its environment, but a supervisor wondered if employees could be counted on to "play" appropriately.

"You give me access to medications that can mean the difference between life and death for patients," a nurse responded. "But you don't trust me to play responsibly?"

Playfulness won't flourish in places where people spend more time trying *not* to do the wrong thing than they do searching for ways to do the right thing. People may "play" in such environments, but they will do it in secret or as a form as rebellion. (Quick, the boss is coming! Get his picture off the dartboard!)

But in healthy workplaces, where people are free to be passionate about their work and accountable to their teammates, play happens naturally. When it happens in a context of "be there," "make their day," and "choose your attitude," play *will* be appropriate and productive.

The following story is about an invitation to play that provided a breath of fresh air in a workplace that needed a little more life. As managers and employees built trust and accountability, people became free to play in a way that lightened their spirits *and* improved the business.

A Company That
Has Fun Connecting:
Sprint Global Connection Services

It seems like just another day at the Sprint Global Connection Services call center in Lenexa, Kansas, but the phone agents are all shook up. There's been an Elvis sighting in the parking lot.

Sure enough, a limousine stops in front of the call center's windows. Aaaaaaaahhhh! (Pause for breath) Aaaaaahhhh! It's the King! Suddenly two Elvi Girls, with poodle skirts, bobby socks, and hair the size of Graceland, rush the King. One attaches herself to his ankles.

Inside the center, grown men and women are so moved by the sight of the King that they are in tears . . . from laughter. "Elvis" looks suspiciously like Don Freeman, manager of Sprint's call center in Phoenix, and one of the Elvi Girls bears a striking resemblance to Mary Hogan, manager of the Lenexa call center.

Lori Lockhart, director of Sprint Global Connection Services, shakes her head in amazement. A few years earlier, who could have believed that managers—you know, the corporate hall monitors—would show up for a meeting dressed like this?

But the customer service agents on the phones are loving every second of it, and though their customers on the other end of the line don't know what's going on, they can hear the enthusiasm and energy in the agents' voices.

As Elvis enters the center, "You ain't nothin' but a hound dog!" wails from the loudspeakers. Lori cringes at the thought of hearing Don—I mean, Elvis—sing. But he decides to lip-synch instead, and after he leaves the building, all Lori can say, in her easy drawl, is, "Thank yuh. Thank yuh very much."

STAYING CONNECTED

Sprint Global Connection Services helps Sprint's long-distance customers get connected around the world. More than 1,000 employees in seven call centers across the country—Sprint has more than 80,000 employees corporate-wide—provide a variety of services, including operator assistance, information, calling cards, prepaid calling cards, customer service for people buying prepaid cards, and directory assistance.

Five years ago, Lori Lockhart wasn't worried about Elvis leaving the building; she was concerned about the agents leaving. "Turnover was becoming a major challenge in our industry, and the long-distance business is so competitive," she says. "We knew if we didn't have a work environment people were excited about, they were going to go elsewhere."

At first glance, *exciting* is not the first word one would use to describe the duties of a call center phone agent. For many it's an entry-level job. Agents handle 500 to 800 calls per day, each one averaging 30 to 35 seconds. Most of the information needed to connect the call is in front of them on a computer screen. "People often master the job so quickly that it can become almost second nature," Mary Hogan says. "You start getting the same kinds of calls over and over, and the boredom factor can set in if you're not careful."

So how do you help employees stay focused through 800 calls a day? In 1997, Sprint thought the answer was to have a lot of rules. "In a competitive, high-pressure environment, there's a tendency to manage by taking over versus letting people do their jobs," Lori says.

Sprint had rules for what its agents could wear. "I can't tell you the number of hours we spent in staff meetings talking about the dress code," Mary says. "How short can a short skirt be? Are women wearing panty hose? You could wear every color of jeans except blue."

Sprint had rules for what you could read. "We knew people could read at their stations and still do a good job," Mary says. "But you could only read Sprint material. You know what happened—people were holding a Sprint publication but inside it was a sports or glamour magazine."

Sprint even had rules for how you could sit. "Ergonomics, you know," Mary says.

"We felt like the police," Lori says. "Instead of finding new ways to make money for the business, we were walking around checking on people all the time."

The more the managers pushed, the more the agents pushed back. According to Lori, "When I had my roundtable meetings with the agents, there was so much nitpicky stuff. *Why can't I put my foot up on the bench? Why can't I wear jeans on Tuesdays, not just Fridays?* I was getting blasted by the agents for things they felt made their environment more stressful."

The managers were feeling stressed too. "It was the way we'd done business for a long time," says Mary, who had been in the call center business since 1964. "We knew we needed to change. We just didn't know how."

In the fall of 1997, Lori and the call center managers attended a Sprint leadership conference. The speaker urged them to find the "radiating possibilities" in each employee. "We were always looking for reasons why people weren't doing their jobs," Lori says. "Why not look for the possibilities instead?"

They also listened to a speaker from Southwest Airlines talking about their famed culture of freedom, teamwork, and respect for individual employees. Five minutes into her speech, the speaker said, "Oh my goodness! Excuse me. I forgot something."

She ducked down behind the podium. When she came back up, she was wearing an inflatable hat shaped like an airplane. She wore it for the rest of her speech. Suddenly Lori, Mary, and the other managers got it: Time to lighten up.

LEAP OF FAITH

Lori and her team began to envision what a workplace looked like where people had fun while they worked hard.

From these discussions they created a culture statement of who they wanted to be:

> We are proud to be a supportive community with a feedback-rich environment that embraces change, values diversity and learns from our experiences. We thrive on creative and innovative ideas, which add value for Sprint customers, employees and shareholders. We achieve our goals because we are accountable for our contributions to Sprint. We have a passion to succeed together and celebrate our accomplishments.

They knew this wasn't going to happen overnight or even in a year; this was going to be a journey of three to five years.

"We didn't tell any of the higher-ups about this," Lori says. "We were going to do it because we knew it was the right thing to do. But I was scared. How was it going to work? Well, it was going to work by delivering results."

Everyone else was scared, too. "We said we're all going to hold hands and jump together," Lori remembers. "Because we needed to have a leap of faith that we're doing the right thing by changing the way we lead."

The team kicked off 1998 by announcing a new dress code: "Just don't wear anything that could be a safety hazard." They also allowed people to read whatever they wanted at their stations.

"The agents used to say we treated them like kids. Our goal was to create an adult environment," Mary says. "You know you are accountable for serving the customer. If you can't do more than one thing at a time, you need to choose not to read. But most agents can do more than one thing at a time, it keeps them engaged through a long day, and they do a better job."

The agents were happier, but Mary was still having trouble getting people to come in on weekends and nights at the call center in Lenexa, a Kansas City suburb, and a satellite center she manages in Kansas City. "People would call in sick during those times," she recalls. "As a result, we were having trouble meeting our goals for service levels, which measure how quickly the average call is answered."

Sprint launched a summer program called Managers Attack Service-Level Headaches (MASH). Late one night Mary and the supervisors decorated the centers like MASH units. They donned khaki shirts at work and provided incentives for working overtime, with Hogan Bucks good for special prizes. IV bottles, attached to overtime sign-up sheets, hung from the ceiling. Supervisors sent candy bars to agents via a remote-control jeep and organized impromptu contests.

People started smiling again and the call centers began to achieve their service-level goals. "We knew we were onto something when I started getting handwritten notes from the agents," says Mary. "They said things like 'I never would have believed in all my years that you would do something this fun for us. Thank you—and don't stop.'

"I think we knew intuitively what needed to be done but didn't have the courage to do it. Those notes gave us the courage."

PLAYING WITH A PURPOSE

When Lori and Mary saw the learning film *FISH!* in the fall of 1998, they turned to each other and said, almost in unison, "That's us!" In a job that could easily have become repetitious and predictable, the fishmongers chose to make it fun and always surprising. They teased customers with a mischievous look that said, "C'mon, tease me back!" Each of the fishmongers acted like an owner of the market. They worked as a team, but as individuals they didn't wait passively to be told what to do. They constantly tried new strategies to engage customers.

When the fishmongers played, it was with a purpose. One second they might be wiggling a fish head at a customer, in the next they were completely focused as that customer placed a large order. The day seemed to breeze by—and they sold a ton of fish.

Had Lori and her team introduced the FISH! Philosophy a few years earlier, the agents might have laughed and said, "OK, what's next?" "Everybody would have thought it was just another flavor of the month," says supervisor Donna Jenkins. "But things had been changing. With every new thing that we added and *didn't* take back, their trust in leadership grew."

First the call centers made FISH! part of their decor. Employees hung posters with the principles everywhere, and supervisors donned fishing vests as a daily reminder of the team's new commitment.

But more important, they made the principles part of their daily lives. "We bought plastic fish stringers and gave one to every employee," Mary recalls. "When supervisors observed agents on the phone demonstrating customer-focused behaviors, they recognized them by giving them fish made out of colored paper. We thought it was important that the supervisors write on the fish exactly what they saw the agent doing, so it reinforced the behavior.

"At the end of each quarter, we held a fishing tournament. We put all the paper fish in a tank. If your name was drawn you got to go fishing for prizes with a pole that had a magnet on the end. People loved it—and they got better at their jobs."

"SIR, THAT CALL IS FREE!"

The centers incorporated the four principles into their regular coaching sessions. "When we want to recognize an agent for great service, we call it a FISH! Tale," Lori explains. "If the customer didn't have a good experience, we call it The One That Got Away."

They look for opportunities to bring a lighter touch to their customer interactions. "One of our agents got a call from a customer wanting to make a collect call to an 800 number," Don explains. "The agent said, 'Sir, today we're going to give you that call for free.'"

They work hard to make the customer's day even when customers are calling with problems. "Our system is pretty automated, and when equipment doesn't work right, it's designed to send the call to our agents," Mary says. "Customers can be pretty unhappy when they call."

When that happens, says agent Rhonda Lynch, "the most important thing is your tone of voice. It's not a fake cheerfulness. It's something sincere in your voice that says, 'I'm really sorry you're having a problem. Let me see what I can do to help you out.'"

When that isn't enough, Sprint's agents choose to stay positive. "Sometimes customers are so upset they don't care how happy you are," says agent Marcia Leibold. "But I'm determined not to let them rile me. I do what I can to help, and by the end of the call, they say, 'You have a good day.'

"Some people call us because they're lonely. Often it's older people, and from something they say, you figure out that they don't have family. While I'm processing the call, they'll want to start up a conversation. From a business perspective I need to get to the next call, but I let them talk a little bit and I try to say something positive to let them know somebody out there cares about them."

And the agents found a way to be there for several hundred calls a day. "Sure, there are days when every call starts to sound the same," Lori says. "But the next call might be someone trying to get through to her grandmother who's ill or a business traveler who misses his wife and kids."

The next call might even be a matter of life or death. "An elderly woman had fallen and couldn't move," Rhonda recalls. "Somehow she got connected to us, but she couldn't dial 911 or tell us where she was. Another agent and I spent 30 minutes making long-distance calls to the police and fire departments in her area—I think it was New York. The other agent talked to her to keep her calm and I placed the calls. Finally we figured out where she was. The police had to break her door down.

"I know we helped saved that lady's life. When I went home that night, I knew I was doing worthwhile work."

HEARING SMILES

At the Lenexa center, Mary and her supervisors continued to look for ways to increase attendance on Friday and Saturday nights. "Many of our employees are 18 to 24 years old," Mary says. "They're the newer employees, so they get hours nobody else wants. We asked ourselves, 'Why wouldn't they want to be here on weekend nights?' Well, duh! They want to be out partying like the rest of the world."

Mary wheeled the stereo system from her office into the call center. "The center is so big we had to crank the speakers," she says, laughing. "At first nobody wanted to sit near the front."

But agents quickly jumped out of their chairs and started boogying while they were processing calls. "Before, if you had a really negative call, you didn't have a release to take your mind off it," explains agent James White. "You'd try but it was hard to shake that feeling for a while. The music gave you something else to focus on for a few seconds, and then you could go on to the next call and give that person your very best."

Mary's team carefully monitored calls during the first few weeks. "We were worried what customers would think of music in the background," she says. "But when we listened, we heard smiles in the agents' voices."

The Lenexa center got only one complaint. A woman called late one Friday night. Midway through the call, she said, "What's going on there? Are you having a party? Let me speak to your supervisor!"

The supervisor came on. "What's going on there?" the woman said suspiciously. "It sounds like a party."

"Yes, ma'am, that's kind of what we're doing," the supervisor said. "We are trying to create a fun atmosphere at work for our agents so they will be here Friday and Saturday nights so they can serve customers like you. I apologize if you don't like the music, but we're just trying to do some things because we care about our employees."

"Are you kidding me?" the woman said. "You'd do that for your employees?" The line was silent for a moment. "That's really nice," she said.

WHAT IF IT DOESN'T WORK?

Had Sprint received a complaint like that two years earlier, Mary says, "we would have apologized all over the place and shut down the whole thing. Heck, we might have shut it down if we had one *internal* complaint."

But part of Sprint's new culture statement talked about "learning from our experiences"—which meant taking risks. "In the past, when we'd talk about trying something new, people would say, 'Now, if this doesn't work, we'll be locked into it forever,'" says Mary. "We didn't want to do anything that could be called a failure, so we never did *anything*.

"Now we said, 'OK, let's call it something else. Let's "pilot" something. Let's "trial" something. It might work and it might not. But if it's something that might improve our culture, let's at least try.'"

Mary brought a toy box into the center, filled with foam discs, foam footballs, and soft toys for people to toss back and forth. "That was a real risk. What if someone gets hurt throwing things around? Now it's a Worker's Comp issue. Then we thought, 'We have established clear accountabilities. They know they have to do their jobs. Why don't we trust them? If something happens, the worst thing is we don't do it again.'

"So now people will sometimes toss stuff back and forth, and the young guys will toss the foam football to keep energized late at night. In three years, we have never had an issue with it. Oh, sometimes the guys get a little rambunctious late at night, but you just settle them down a bit."

The same thing happened when Mary installed a big-screen TV in the Lenexa center. "It makes it nice for the football and basketball fans working weekends. The first weekend the TV was in, one of the agents brought in a video.

"On Monday morning I came in and opened an e-mail that basically said, 'Oh Mary, we know we're in big trouble. We showed the movie and it had a scene that wasn't appropriate for the center and now we can't watch videos anymore!' I just laughed and told them, 'Well, I guess we'll be screening movies now.'

"In a positive work environment, it's not about taking

things away. It's about learning every day and finding solutions that allow people to have an energized culture."

Music is a big part of that culture now. "We decided we didn't want elevator music. We wanted upbeat music. But people have different tastes. We bought a bunch of CDs, almost every style, and told the agents, 'We're going to play your kind of music, but we're also going to play *other* people's music. That way it's something we can all enjoy.' It was a good way of teaching diversity."

STARTING RUMORS

In Sprint's more straitlaced days, the call centers occasionally tried to have fun. "We'd send out formal communications," Lori says. "We'd say, 'Hey, a fun thing is coming! We're gonna have fun Friday at 1 p.m.!'" The message, of course, was that it wasn't fun the rest of the time.

But at Sprint's call centers, it became increasingly difficult to predict what might happen, especially on Friday and Saturday nights. And the managers and supervisors led the way. On New Year's Eve, Mary showed up dressed like a baby. Sometimes she led agents in the Chicken Dance or Macarena. "If customers could have seen the weird stuff we were doing while processing their calls, they wouldn't have believed it," she says. "On the other hand, most of them probably would have joined in!" (The Chicken Dance eventually died a natural death. "People got tired of it. Maybe it's time for a comeback," she says with a wink.)

"Every week a new rumor would start up," Lori says. "The young agents would tell each other, 'Make sure you're working this weekend, because something crazy might happen.'"

One weekend Mary hung a small disco ball from the ceiling. All weekend the agents processed calls while listening to the likes of the Bee Gees and KC and the Sunshine Band and doing the Hustle. The weekend was such a hit that Mary installed two larger disco balls. "They don't rotate all the time," she says. "If we're a little sluggish, we turn off the lights, turn on the balls, and crank the music."

Sometimes the agents played bingo, with supervisors walking around displaying the numbers on a board. "When someone gets bingo, the supervisor takes 15 minutes of calls for them while they take a break," Mary says. "It's a good way for supervisors to keep up their call-processing skills."

At Sprint's call center in Jacksonville, Florida, one of the supervisors created a character called "Delightful Day." At least once a month she visited each customer agent station with her shocking outfits and greeting of "Helllewwwwww!" On July 4, Delightful Day showed up in a blue sequin dress with red trim and flags hanging from her hat.

All this activity occasionally made the managers nervous. One night at the Phoenix center, about 10 p.m., there was so much going on that Don Freeman became concerned that customers were hearing this. "So I started monitoring calls from my office," he says. "I listened to call after call and I got goosebumps.

"I wasn't hearing any of the craziness in the background. I

wasn't hearing lifeless, monotone "SprintmayIhelpyou" voices, either. I was hearing energized, alive 'Sprint! May I *help* you?' voices. It was so awesome I went down to the center floor and joined in."

Don began making regular appearances as Elvis with his guitar, while the agents pleaded with him not to quit his day job. He also redesigned the Phoenix center's physical environment to resemble a coffeehouse, with couches, pool tables, and high-speed Internet access, to appeal to the Arizona State students who made up a large part of their workforce. "A lot of the students come in early to work now just to hang out," Don says.

What might have happened at Sprint's call centers if leadership had only told people to play, instead of playing along with them? "We would have tried, but we would have always been looking over our shoulder, wondering, 'Are we going back to the old days?'" Rhonda says. "Sometimes when we get real busy, we don't have a lot of time to play, but at least we know it's not going away."

"IT'S NICE TO KNOW YOU'RE HUMAN!"

Part of creating a more adult atmosphere at Sprint's call centers was to give people choices. That meant giving people the choice *not* to play. "Sometimes people have a headache, don't like the music, or they want to study while they process calls," Mary says. "We have a separate room across the hall from the main center where there's no music or activities." Agents can go back and forth at any time during the day.

"Some of our folks feel if you're working hard, you shouldn't be having fun. It may be generational or just the way they were raised. Others say, 'This is cool,'" says Lori. "But it's not about having to participate in the music or games. For some people it's knitting something for your grandchild or your neighbor's baby, or drawing something you love—whatever it is that brings you joy so you can transfer that feeling to the customer.

"And if a supervisor hears a perfect call, they'll run out and do something zany and immediately recognize the agent. The other agents see it and are celebrating each other's success while still taking calls—which brings a smile when they're talking to the customer."

It's also about being yourself when you serve others. Each of the call centers do monthly quality surveys with agents to make sure their interactions with customers are up to expectations. "We used to have a form with dozens of questions, like 'How many times did you say please and thank you?'" Mary says. "If you didn't say thank you a certain number of times, we'd take points off. That really bugged the agents. They'd say, 'You are so nitpicky.'"

Sprint sought feedback from agents on the elements that comprised a great call and streamlined the form. "We still want people to be polite," says Mary. "But now we try to find opportunities to play or be there, instead of demanding automatic responses that may not always be appropriate."

In the process, Sprint replaced robot-like sameness with authenticity and individuality. "Sometimes we'll be laughing about something crazy, like Mary walking by wearing a pig nose," Marcia says, "and the customer will say, 'It's nice to know you're human!'"

MOMMY, WHY ARE YOU ACTING SO FUNNY?

One day, while attending Sprint's annual leadership conference, Lori Lockhart had an epiphany. She was having fun. She had dressed like a fish at a conference. She danced with Elvis and the Elvi Girls. "I finally felt comfortable that I could be myself," she explains. "I became more relaxed, more confident in my leadership abilities. I was having fun seeing results."

Then it hit her. "I'm living the FISH! Philosophy at work," she thought. "Why don't I take it home to my family?"

The first night she came home she decided to play, have fun, and be there instead of being tired, stressed, and irritable. "My daughters immediately saw this change in me. They said, 'Mommy, why are you acting so funny?'

"I told them, 'This is the new me and I'll try harder to be a better mommy and have more fun.' They told me that they thought I was wonderful before, but now I was the best mom in the universe!"

The next morning (this part of the day was typically filled with stress, sometimes tears, and always racing the clock), Lori tried to start the day with humor and play as she prepared for work. As her daughters walked her out to the car for the morning good-bye ritual, they had big grins on their faces and said, "Because of Mommy, it's going to be a great day and we're going to have fun today."

"Those words made my day," Lori says. "We really try not to sweat the small stuff. The other day my husband, Patrick, told me he was going to start choosing his attitude and dance while he's vacuuming. Great, honey, go for it."

CREATING OWNERSHIP, STIMULATING CREATIVITY

Sprint's call centers have always had an open-door policy. "But it didn't always feel like open door," agent Rhonda Lynch remembers, laughing. She holds her thumb and forefinger less than an inch apart. "It was open door . . . to a point."

Today, agents are an integral part of how the call centers plan. "We decided before launching any major changes we would do our homework and engage employees in those discussions," says Mary.

Each of the call centers has widely used feedback channels. Lori even has her own online feedback site. "I ask people to please tell me if something I'm doing is not living up to our culture." The feedback can be blunt, as when an agent told her to communicate more clearly and concisely. "I need that. I can't take action on something I'm not aware of."

Agents also play a major role in identifying opportunities for better performance. "Three years ago, I would have never had an agent come to me to present a new idea to improve a business result," says Lori. "Now I have meeting after meeting with agent teams who are presenting proposals on how we can improve call-handling efficiencies or customer satisfaction. Some of those proposals have saved big dollars."

In Phoenix, Don Freeman regularly invites agents to act as "Sprint board members" and tell him what they think the call center should be working on.

Leadership also has moved to more of an open-book management philosophy. "I talk a lot with employees about the challenges that keep me up at night," Lori says. "We talk about budgets, unit-cost targets, margin challenges, competition."

A few years ago, Lori believes, the agents wouldn't have cared. "Now there's a much keener interest at all levels of the organization in how the metrics work together—financial, customer satisfaction, employee performance. People understand how what they do every day helps to drive the business."

In the process, by playing with ideas, Sprint's employees unleashed a lot of unexplored creativity. "A lot of people don't think they have that ability," says Mary. "But once you realize we're not going to put limits on your mind, that we want you to brainstorm with us, you would be amazed what opens up. People who I never would have dreamed were creative have come up with wonderful ideas—and I think they've surprised themselves too."

And the more management and employees play together, the more barriers go down.

According to Lori: "It all builds confidence in people that 'If I say something to Lori or Mary or one of the supervisors, they will listen to me and do something, and if they can't, they'll tell me why.'"

"As supervisors, we really are committed to being fully present for each and every employee," Donna Jenkins adds.

"It feels like a family," says agent Marcia Leibold. "I feel more connected to the management team than I ever have."

That trust will be key to the future. "There is so much change going on," says Mary. "It used to be that every time we wanted to make a change, we had to go through these huge change-management cycles. For employees it can be like a grief cycle. We don't have time for these lengthy change cycles anymore. The more trust we build with employees, the more they feel confident about the quick shifts we may need to make."

In October 1999, Sprint and MCI WorldCom began merger talks. "The day of the announcement, our leadership team watched the business news with agents on our big-screen TV," says Mary. "We talked a lot with employees about what was happening."

The merger eventually fell through. But what really impressed Mary was the reaction of the agents. "Had this happened a few years earlier, there would have been so much fear. But because of the trust that had been built up, there was a calmness that boggled my mind."

AN ANSWER FOR "HMMM"

The first time Gary Owens, Sprint's vice president of service operations, visited the Lenexa call center after Mary had installed disco balls, a speaker system, and a big-screen TV, she stopped him as they were about to go into the center: "I said, 'Gary, I need to tell you about some changes we've made so you don't have a mild coronary.' He walked in and all he kept saying was, 'Hmmm . . . hmmm . . . hmmm.'"

Then Mary showed him the call center's numbers. It had met or exceeded every one of its goals for retention, service levels, productivity, customer satisfaction, and on and on. "If you had ever asked me about putting in disco balls, I would have said, 'No way,'" he told Mary months later. "But you can't argue with success."

Having recognized the success, Gary endorsed the approach for the entire organization, using Lori's team as an internal benchmark. Gary also changed the organization's vision statement to *We have fun working while delivering the ideal customer experience in consumer communications.*

The numbers for all of Sprint Global Connection Services were becoming more impressive. The first year they went after a 25 percent increase in retention and exceeded it. Since then they've maintained it.

"We've actually had folks looking at higher-paying jobs within Sprint and turning them down because they liked our environment so much," Mary says.

Call center productivity, which was already high, increased another 20 percent from 1997 to 2001, and Sprint's call centers won a number of customer satisfaction awards. The group sets tougher and tougher goals each year. "We've met all of them," Mary says.

But Mary had another way of assessing her call center's

progress. "Before, I would walk down the hallways and hear little complaints here and there. I'd see people frowning. When you see and hear that stuff all the time, you tend to filter it out and don't pay as much attention to it as you should.

"But as our culture changed, people became happier, upbeat, relaxed. When I walk down the hallways now and I see a frown or there's even a hint that a person has a complaint or problem, my radar goes up right away. I know it's not normal anymore. I deal with the issue immediately, which just means our workplace is going to be better."

LIVING THE PHILOSOPHY

Mary Hogan used to just carry reports. Now she has a bag of props. "Every morning when I walk through the center it's like I'm going on stage," she says. "You never know when I might walk out in pig slippers or kitten slippers or crank the music or grab somebody off their position and start dancing.

"I've been in the call center business 37 years and I am living proof that you can change. My management style today is nothing like it was a few years ago. The change has allowed me to show my human side to everybody. I am who I am and people can see it now. They can hear it too—because I'm usually laughing."

Mary has had opportunities to move into higher positions. "But I can't make myself move on. The past few years have been the most energizing of my career. I have so much passion for what we're doing.

"We have crossed so many lines. I don't know if there are any lines we *wouldn't* cross to try to improve the business. But when you launch on journeys, you have to get outside your comfort zone. It's not about seeking permission. We all have a certain sphere of influence. It's about taking risks within that sphere.

"It feels like *Star Trek*. We're boldly going where no one else has gone before."

SMALL BITES

✂ MEMORIES ✂

Is there any workplace where you *can't* play? How about a funeral home? Yet we heard this story from a funeral director: A family was sitting at the funeral home, lost in their grief. The funeral director suggested that they all join him in a circle and talk about the fun times they had had with their mother. Before long, laughter mixed with tears as they celebrated the joy and happiness she had brought into their lives.

✂ THE LIGHTHEARTED TOUCH OF A CHILD ✂

Why do so many flip charts have to look so boring? One woman decided to spice up her presentation by asking her kids to color her flip charts with crayons. Her coworkers loved the rainbow-splashed flip charts, and her playful presentation was a hit.

꓿ **THE WIGGLE FACTOR** ꓿

As John Christensen was about to pay for his purchases at a large discount store, he reached for the pen-on-a-chain to sign his check. Suddenly the pen wiggled out of his reach. The cashier was pulling on the end of the chain hidden underneath the counter. John laughed. So did the cashier. Every time John goes into one of these stores now, he hopes he'll be as engaged and delighted as he was by that cashier. Just in case, he also carries his own pen.

꓿ **FUN IS FUNDAMENTAL** ꓿

A new hospital, inspired by the fishmongers, decided to integrate play into its basic philosophy. Part of its mission statement reads, "We are dedicated to exceeding our customers' expectations in a compassionate and *fun* atmosphere." Its core values include quality, compassion, integrity, organized solid planning, teamwork, and *fun*.

Play and productivity go hand in hand in this hospital. On Beach Party Day, patients who are able toss a beach ball to each other. Little do they know this is physical therapy. If they were in the therapy room, they might not give much effort. The fun factor changes everything.

꓿ **LIGHT UP SOME SMILES** ꓿

Sure, "play" sounds great. But what if your workplace is a heavy manufacturing plant where safety is critical? First, any activity that puts someone at risk is *not* play. It's recklessness. But there are ways to lighten spirits even in the most demanding environments. During December at a tool manufacturing plant, the maintenance workers hung icicle lights on the chainlink fence surrounding the site. The machine operators asked if they could decorate too if they kept it safe. Garlands and twinkle lights began to appear wrapped around workbenches and conduit—anything that didn't move.

Play doesn't have to be a specific activity; sometimes it's a state of mind. And a state of mind is influenced by the environment you create.

⤬ WHO AM I TODAY? ⤬

Interviews are often intimidating, uncomfortable, and a good way to ruin the armpits of your best shirt. But an employment consultant at a major university has found a way to bring play into the process. She comes dressed according to the position for which the applicant is applying. If people are interviewing for construction jobs, she dresses as a construction worker, hard hat and all. If people are interviewing for security jobs, she dresses as a security guard. It puts the applicants at ease, introduces them to a culture of fun—and attracts people who will flourish there.

⤬ THE DECIDING FACTOR ⤬

Every company wants to attract the best employees, but you'd be surprised what draws them. A young computer talent chose his company because a miniature blimp was flying around the office when he interviewed there. The salary and benefits were competitive; he figured it would be more fun and professionally stimulating to work there.

"IF YOU'D LIKE TO HEAR A DUCK QUACK, PRESS 7...."

What can you do to attract employees? At one company, employees decorate job applications with crayons and welcome notes. Another company encourages employees to record entertaining phone messages, then suggests that potential hires call random staff numbers after hours to get a feel for how much fun it is to work there.

A BIGGER PLAYING FIELD

Before they felt it was safe to play, the employees of a large ski resort wanted to know how far they could go. "They wanted to know how big the playing field is," the CEO told us. "'If we step off the playing field you can call foul, but let's together define the size of the playing field.' I started with a relatively tight playing field—these are the rules. The employees said, 'No, we need an expanded playing field—expanded rules, a little more latitude, a little more trust.'"

So the CEO redrew the lines and made the playing field bigger. Now the resort holds impromptu karaoke contests on the mountains. Kids bob for crawdads. Guests do the limbo on their way to the chairlifts. Every ski resort in the area has the same beautiful mountains and amenities. This resort is trying to differentiate itself by freeing its people to create more playful, personalized experiences for its guests. How big is your playing field? Does it need to grow?

Section Two—MAKE THEIR DAY

*The world becomes a better place the moment you act on
an intention to serve another.*

When you first walk into the World Famous Pike Place Fish market, you might think you are being entertained. The flying fish, shouts, chants, teasing of customers, and antics are entertaining. But you come to realize that you have walked onto a stage and have become a member of the cast. The fish guys are sizing you up and just waiting for an opportunity to throw you a line. They are committed to recreating their vision of the market each day. But that can only happen if they find a way to make a memory for you so that when you leave, whether you are carrying a fish or not, you leave with something you will want to share with others. Then those others will themselves come to the market. And they too will leave with a memory. More will come. The word will spread as the ripples go out. And more will come. . . . You get the picture.

At the center of the incredible success of Pike Place Fish is the engagement of one person at a time. It bears repeating.

They are not selling fish; they are making the world a better place to live, one engagement at a time. By the way, they sell a lot of fish.

An opportunity arose one day to introduce a friend and supporter to the market. I had heard he would be in Seattle on business and suggested he make his first visit the market while in town.

At about 3:45 on a Thursday afternoon, Ken arrived at the market and stood in the back row enjoying the energy and the action. A thought crossed his mind and his face must have telegraphed it ever so slightly. It was the only opening Sammy needed as he approached Ken and said, "May I help you?"

"I was thinking that smoked salmon would be great at a family get-together this weekend. What would you suggest?"

"I think you should sample a couple different kinds," suggested Sammy.

Five minutes and three kinds of salmon later, Sammy asked for a commitment and Ken made his choice, decided on an amount, and gave Sammy his credit card. Sammy went back to the credit card machine gingerly holding the card. A moment later he returned with a serious, concerned look. "Do you have another card, Ken?"

Ken experienced an unusual emotion; he was flustered, and he frantically searched for cash or another card. After he had dug in his pockets for what must have seemed an eternity, Sammy spoke up.

"I was just curious, Ken. I don't need one."

Ken was so caught up in the moment that he missed this cue. Finally Sammy said, "I don't need another credit card, Ken. I just wondered if you had one."

Ken's face broke into a giant grin. He had just experienced a playful engagement and a lasting memory was formed. The ripples go out from that moment every time Ken tells that story. Listeners smile when they hear it and many find their way to the market to collect their own memories. And the ripples go out in larger numbers. And people come to the market to collect their own stories. And on and on . . .

After Ken left the market we told the guys that it was Ken Blanchard, author of many best-selling business books including *The One-Minute Manager*. They said, "Who is Ken Blanchard?" They had simply treated him the way they treat any willing customer.

There is nothing quite as powerful as turning your attention away from yourself and asking how you might connect with another human being, customer, family member, or colleague and "make their day." Or as Justin at the market says, "At least make their moment."

The next story is about a car dealership committed to making each customer visit a memorable one. That's not an easy task, given the way many people feel about having to haggle over a vehicle. But it became a task transformed once the employees of Rochester Ford Toyota began a journey to discover how to focus on other people's needs, not their own.

Driven to Serve Others:
Rochester Ford Toyota

The lot at Rochester Ford Toyota is filled with hundreds of vehicles, but right now Rob Gregory is interested in just one: a NASCAR racing car that's visiting his car dealership as part of a promotion. "Just listen to that," he says lovingly as its engine roars.

For a few seconds, Rob is the boy from Grand Forks, North Dakota, who used to love shopping for cars with his father. "I thought it was the best thing in the world," he says.

As he grew up, he learned that many people felt differently. "If it's a choice between getting teeth pulled and buying a car, the dentist gets the first call."

But when Rob first took a job selling cars in Grand Forks in 1987, he met a man with a different vision. Wes Rydell's western jackets and bandana neckties gave him the appearance of a Hollywood cowboy, and his maverick ideas set him apart from the herd. "His vision went something like this: 'Do the exact opposite of what the rest of our industry is doing and you'll be close,'" Rob recalls.

"Mr. Rydell talked about being a 10, reaching your fullest

potential. People want to be a 10. They want their marriage to be a 10. Companies want to be a 10. From a business perspective, how do you start on that path?

"Mr. Rydell believed there are five areas essential to every business's success: 1) Customer enthusiasm, 2) Employee satisfaction, 3) Ability to generate profits, 4) Growing market, and 5) Continuous improvement. All five are necessary conditions, but you can only pick one as your favorite."

Most car dealerships chose to be driven by 3—profits—but Rydell decided to focus on 1—customer enthusiasm. "Any one of these isn't necessarily better or worse than any other is," Rob says. "But when you focus on customers first, it puts you on a different journey. You stop focusing on what *you* want and start focusing on what the people you are serving want.

"Mr. Rydell said, 'When a friend of mind comes in, I make sure they get the best deal possible. What would happen if I treated every customer as if they were my friend?'"

From this perspective, Rydell created a new vision for his dealerships: *To Be So Effective That We Are Able to Be Helpful to Others*. "If you get really good at what you do, who would come to you to be served?" Rob asks. "Everybody would. The more people you are truly serving, how do you feel? You feel great!

"Yes, you need to stay focused on profit. But is it a cause or an effect? If you ask people if they want to be a millionaire, everyone says yes. But if you ask *why* they want to be a millionaire, the underlying reason always comes down to this: They want to be happy. The only way to be happy in this life is to get outside yourself and serve others. That's the journey Mr. Rydell was trying to get me on."

WHAT ARE YOU FEEDING?

When Rob bought Universal Ford Toyota in Rochester, Minnesota, in November 1999, many employees weren't feeling especially happy.

"It had a reputation as a typical car dealership—come in, get beat up," recalls Al Utesch, Universal's parts manager for several years. "Most people worked hard for the customer, but the main goal was financial. Our customer satisfaction scores were among the worst in our region, and employee satisfaction was so low it was almost immeasurable."

"I saw a lot of people pay high prices, and those who didn't negotiated until they were blue in the face," says John Davids, who had joined the sales staff six months before Rob purchased the dealership.

Even the dealership's profitability was misleading. The economy had been robust for several years and Rochester— home of the Mayo Clinic, one of the world's leading medical centers—was a prosperous community. "The previous ownership would have given itself an A in profitability, but in terms of the market's potential, it was really a C," Rob says.

Rob was not surprised, but neither was he judgmental. "Ownership chose to emphasize 3 (profit), not 1 (customer satisfaction)," he said. "The owner lived out of town and saw the dealership as an investment, not a mission. If you lived out of town and got a big check every month, what would you change?"

But when you build an environment based on take, that's what you feed in even well-intentioned people. Customers come in with their defenses up. Salespeople try to make as much as they can on each car because they think they might never see the customer again. Management tries to squeeze profits from every corner, and employees focus on what they can get, not on what they can give.

The dealership's decision to run sales, service, and parts as three distinct financial entities created—unintentionally—an environment in which coworkers saw each other as competitors. "With the emphasis on the bottom line, we blamed each other for everything," says Julie Sweningson, parts manager. "It got so bad that we would refer our friends to other dealerships if they wanted to buy a car, and sales would refer their customers to other parts stores because they said we were difficult to work with."

No one, including ownership, felt good about the situation, but no one knew quite how to change it. Profits seemed good and, as Wes Rydell had said, your focus determines the way you see the world.

"I talked to a lot of people individually when we came, and there was some drama, some victim language," remembers Brian Kopek, who moved to Rochester Ford Toyota with Rob as new-car sales manager. "If we had a rallying cry, it would have been, 'I'm gonna get mine.'"

Rob made one major external change, renaming the dealership "Rochester Ford Toyota," but he told the employees that the most important change needed was an internal one.

"How is everything working for us?" Rob asked. "If we keep doing what we're doing, will things get better or worse?"

The answer was almost unanimous: "Worse."

"And how is everything working for you personally? Is your work doing for you what you hoped it would?"

The room was quiet.

Rob called for a new journey. "What if we put the customer's needs before our needs?" he said. "What does the customer really want?"

Do they want to negotiate with several people to get the lowest price or do they want to know our price up front? Up front. "OK, no more negotiating or pressure tactics," Rob said. "We'll post our best possible price on every vehicle. It'll be like playing poker with our cards showing; we'd better have a pretty good hand."

And does the customer ever want to buy a bad car? No. "OK, anyone who buys a used car from us gets their money back in seven days," Rob said. "If they bring it back within 30 days, they can exchange it for any used vehicle of equal or greater value."

Does the customer want to deal with salespeople who are paid to sell or paid to serve? Paid to serve. "OK, our salespeople will be paid per each unit sold, not a percentage of what they negotiate on each vehicle."

By lowering the price of each vehicle, Rob was asking his staff to sell twice as many cars for the same amount of money.

"You can either try to make a lot on a little, or a little on a lot," he said. "I believe it was Sam Walton who said, 'A little bit on a lot is *still* a lot.'"

But all Rob's staff heard him saying was, "We're going to work twice as hard, and we might go broke, and you might make the same salary—I think you'll actually make more—but you *could* get happy along the way!"

Only a few employees liked the sound of that. Most held their breath and waited to see what would happen. Some quit.

A PHILOSOPHY, NOT A PROGRAM

Had any business succeeded by focusing on what Rob was asking of his employees? Well, yes, he explained, a fish market had.

He told them the story of Pike Place Fish and its vision of becoming world famous. The fishmongers didn't get into that journey simply because they wanted to sell more fish. They just wanted to be happier. When they looked outside of themselves and concentrated on helping other people, they discovered a satisfaction they had not imagined possible. As they served more people, more people came to them to be served. How did they feel? They felt great.

Some employees at Rochester Ford Toyota thought what the fishmongers were doing was amazing—exactly what they had been looking for. Some thought it was amusing. Some thought it was obvious. Some thought it was BS.

"To most people it looked a lot better than their current

reality," Rob says. "So we had a choice. Should we take some personal responsibility and try to change our environment, or should we keep waiting for the solution to arrive on a silver platter?"

Initially they threw stuff to each other, joked with customers, did ballet moves across the showroom floor—"anything to add levity to drudgery," Rob says. "Obviously the old way wasn't working and people were willing to listen. Plus when you own the place, some people will pretend to care even if they don't."

"The excitement seemed to be there, mostly in the showroom, but I think some people were still terrified, so whatever leadership did, they were going to do," Brian recalls.

A few months after assuming ownership of the dealership, Rob attended an employee culture meeting. "I'm thinking 1-2-3-4-5 is working, the whole thing is working, and a few people said, 'Do you realize nothing has really changed around here?'

"Well, some things were changing. But if from your point of view it hasn't changed, you haven't changed. So they were actually confessing that they hadn't changed. Basically they were saying, 'One more time, Rob, let me get this straight: I have to sell twice as many cars to make the same salary . . . but I'm going to feel better? It doesn't feel too good today!'"

Rob realized at that moment that the journey was just beginning. He had thought 1-2-3-4-5 and the FISH! Philosophy would fix everything and everyone—instantly. "But nothing gets fixed until we choose to fix ourselves. They had implemented all kinds of programs at the store to try to fix it, but they came and went. That's what people thought this was."

Rob saw that these principles are a philosophy, not a program. A philosophy is not implemented; it is explored, chosen, believed, and practiced. Some people at the dealership were already practicing these principles; for others the decision to embrace them might come 10 minutes later, a month later, maybe even years later.

"If you give a squirt gun to people who don't trust you, then say, 'Have fun!', of course they're going to think you're full of it. First we needed to build trust and accountability. People need to see you are committed to something more than just a program of the month."

Not long after, Rob was looking at copy for two proposed billboards, both of them standard brand messages, such as One Low Price! "I was trying to decide between the two, and it popped into my head. In 10 seconds I drew it out: 'Have You Tried Our Fish?'"

A few managers were helping Rob select the final billboard. They saw the first two billboard ideas. No and no.

"Check this out," Rob said. He showed them what he had just drawn.

They all pointed to it and said, "That's it!"

"WE ACTUALLY HAD FUN. . . ."

Rochester Ford Toyota's new billboard went up, just across the highway from the dealership, in March 2000. The first day a woman called and asked what kind of fish they were selling; Brian started thinking they should put a small case of salmon in the dealership.

Some people were suspicious. "Customers would call up and say, 'What does that mean? Is there something fishy going on? Are you trying to fish us in?'" recalls sales associate Sam Grosso.

The sales staff hadn't paid much attention to the billboard. But the prospect of customers descending on the showroom asking about this cryptic message suddenly commanded their attention. "How are we supposed to respond to that?" they said.

But when they thought through it, it wasn't that hard. "What works in the fish business works in the car business," Sam says. "Serve people, make it fun, have a good attitude, be there when you're needed. Most people understood that."

The hardest part was convincing customers that Rochester Ford Toyota was serious: the price on the car *was* actually the price. "People come in prepared for battle and there is no battle," Sam says.

One by one, several of the salespeople started to let go of their fear. It wasn't easy, but they stopped thinking about the money and started thinking about the other person's needs. Selling a car stopped being a chess match in which each player tried to anticipate the other's next move, and became a conversation about the customer's needs.

Customers noticed. "Before, you'd get lines from the salesman like, 'Now, I wouldn't do this for everybody,'" a customer said on the showroom floor one day. "Yeah, right. I can just hear the salesman thinking, 'Because out of the 30,000 people I see each year, sir, I can honestly tell you that *you* are special.'

"But there was none of that here. They explained all of the options and additional coverage with absolutely no exaggerating attempts to make you feel you should get it. Just 'Here are the advantages. Here are the disadvantages. Let me know how I can help.' I was here when it was Universal, and I can tell you, it's an entirely different place."

Soon customers started writing letters that said things like: "We actually had fun purchasing this car."

"Provided me with the service and kindness of a friend. . . ."

"Being a widow, I did wonder how you would treat me. I received top attention, indicating I was important. . . ."

"I had commented with my coworkers about the car-shopping experience—just wishing and wanting the effort to be straightforward, honest, pleasant, and short-lived. Then I came on a fluke to Rochester Ford Toyota and found the characteristics I thought could not exist. . . ."

"I'm young and female, but I was treated with complete and total respect. . . ."

"This is the best car-buying experience I have ever had, and I have probably bought 25 to 30 vehicles in my lifetime."

Months earlier, when Rob had introduced the new commission approach, several members of the sales force, Sam Grosso included, had thought seriously about leaving. Some top producers did. But Rob convinced those who stayed to give him six months, and their sales increased dramatically. "It worked," Sam says. "It just makes things easier when you're not worrying if people think they got a good deal or they got the same deal as their neighbor. I'm having a good time now. My old customers see the difference in me."

One day Rob stopped by to say hello to a customer—a large, intimidating man—who was completing a purchase with salesman Howard Hawk. "I hate car dealers," the man growled, then smiled. "This will be the first place I ever bought a car without having to cuss somebody out."

SELLING WHAT THEY NEED

Not long after, the staff watched a video featuring John Miller on personal accountability. In it Miller told how he once requested lemonade in a restaurant. "I'm sorry," the young waiter said, "we don't sell lemonade." Five minutes later the waiter placed a glass of lemonade on Miller's table.

Miller was confused. "I thought you didn't sell lemonade."

"We don't," the waiter responded, grinning. "I sent my manager to a store around the corner to get it for you."

A few days later a customer came into the Rochester Ford Toyota showroom. One of the salespeople asked if he'd like something to drink. "What I'd really like is a cappuccino," the man said jokingly.

"We didn't have cappuccino," Rob says. "So our salesperson says to himself, 'Let's see if this is for real.' While he showed the customer around, one of the other guys drove over to a convenience store, grabbed a cappuccino, and brought it back for him."

The customer couldn't believe it. And he bought a car. But all the sales staff could talk about was the delighted look on the customer's face.

Skilled salespeople have always known how to make customers comfortable. "How could I ask you for a big profit over dealer cost and get you to buy from me, unless you laughed or I somehow got you to enjoy the process?" says sales associate Dan Kocer.

But a shift began to happen. "Now when you talk to people, the first thing in your mind isn't how much money am I going to make on this customer because I need to make a house payment," Dan says. "You know something's going to come out of it—if not a relationship, then at least a better feeling about how you're treating people."

The true test came when people automatically started doing what they didn't need to do. Instead of just pointing people to the parts department, they escorted them there. Instead of leaving the customer in a room alone while they checked out her trade-in, they invited her to ride along. When they saw a mother simultaneously coping with a fussy baby and trying to find the service department for an oil change, they volunteered to drive her truck there and get the process started.

John Davids tried to make people's day by doing things for which he didn't get paid, like making sure accessories were added so the vehicle was ready when the customer wanted it. "It all starts with attitude," he says. "Even helpful, good-natured people need to check their attitudes every day, because it's easy to worry about the money first. Just be willing to come in and serve every day. We can actually build friendships now. The other day a customer from out of town invited me to dinner. How can you beat that?"

"It's not everybody's thing, but when some people pick up their vehicles, we make it an event. We have all the salespeople step out and give a round of applause; everybody thanks them, we give them roses and balloons," Brian Kopek says. "And people cry. My gosh! How do you explain that?

"When you're in business every day, you tend to think, 'It's *just* a car!' Maybe they've been treated terribly in the past. We need to remember that we're selling people something they need for their lives. They need that car to go to the hospital, to go on vacation, to pick their kids up from school.

"When customers get emotional like that, Rob will get a little choked up. He has to walk away. He'll say, 'I think I saw some garbage on the lot. I better go pick it up.'"

LITTLE THINGS

If you look up the word *calm* in the dictionary, you'll find Lloyd Hyberger's picture. "I'm pretty easygoing," he says. "I don't get too worked up about anything."

Maybe that's why Lloyd, a sales associate at Rochester Ford Toyota, doesn't mind lending his car to customers whose own vehicles are in the shop. "If a customer is in a pinch I sometimes let them take my personal vehicle to work. They bring it back when they pick up their car. If something happens, that's what insurance is for.

"I'm a pretty relaxed guy, and I want other people to feel relaxed. I've got a little fan in my office and if somebody comes in on a hot day, I turn it in their direction a bit to take the sweat off their brow."

The mercury was considerably lower one night when Lloyd got a call at the showroom. "It was pretty bitter, a typical Minnesota winter night," he remembers. The caller lived in Dubuque, Iowa, but she was staying at a hotel a few miles away near the Mayo Clinic, where her husband was receiving leukemia treatments.

The woman's car was already in the Rochester Ford Toyota shop for repairs. She was worried enough about her husband; she was tired of worrying about their car. "I want to look for a new car," she said.

Lloyd told her to take a taxi. He said he'd pay for it. He warmed up a car and drove her around the lot until she found the vehicle she wanted. "We had already appraised her other car. We cleaned up the new car for her, transferred her belongings from her old car. She wasn't sure how to get back to the hotel, so I drew her a little map." By the time Lloyd was finished, it was more than an hour past closing time.

The woman returned the next day. She was not alone. She had told her husband about how she had been treated, and he had left his hospital bed because he wanted to thank Lloyd.

Several weeks later Lloyd got a letter from the woman. "When my courageous husband was fighting leukemia at Mayo and our car broke down, you treated me so honestly and compassionately that my husband wanted to meet you," she wrote. "He shook your hand one month before he died."

"We just did what we were supposed to do," Lloyd says. "But I sure felt good about it." His quiet voice softens even more. "Gosh, I think about that just about every day."

CHANGE YOURSELF

Even as the environment at Rochester Ford Toyota changed, there were days when Rob wanted it to change even faster. "I love quick fixes. It's part of my nature as a human being. I want what I want when I want it," he says. "See, one of my frustrations is that I think I have this gift: I can see what's wrong with everyone else.

"But if you want to change the world, first you have to change yourself. That has been very humbling, because I realized that nine out of ten problems in my organization, it's always been me. Now I see that. So as I work on myself, I find I have a bigger impact than when I was trying to work on other people."

So Rob worked on himself. He began to learn to listen. "There are times when Rob doesn't like what you have to say about how he's handled a situation or talked to someone, but he will reflect on it, come back, and sincerely be appreciative," says Al Utesch.

He began to learn to give his employees freedom. "Deep down, if I'm honest with myself, I know I still measure things by money," Rob notes. "So when people make decisions that have financial repercussions, it's difficult for me not to shoot the messenger or fire at will.

"But we have a card with our values on it, and it says, 'We have nothing of greater value than our people.' So what does that look like in practice? Would you be patient while your employees learned if you truly valued people? The answer is, 'Of course.'"

Rob also learned, more and more, to be led by the organization's vision, not short-term considerations. "One of Lloyd's customers calls us up," he recalls. "He's going out to Idaho. The truck he bought from us is acting up in a blizzard in South Dakota. He's at another dealership and he says they can't fix it today. I said, 'If they can't, pick a vehicle on their lot, load your stuff in it, and I'll just buy it from them for you when you get back.' Well, the dealer fixed the truck; I think they saw how committed we were and their pride got involved.

"That guy didn't just buy a vehicle from us. He bought our reputation."

JUMPING IN WITH BOTH FEET

As Rob started changing himself, others decided to join him on that lifelong journey—people like Al Utesch. The parts manager, who had started out washing cars at the dealership 29 years earlier, had thought about leaving. But there was something in this belief about getting outside yourself that sounded a lot like what his parents had taught him and what he was teaching his own children.

Then the service manager resigned. Rob felt Al was the best candidate for the job, though not everyone else did—Al included. "After 29 years in parts, I was in a comfort zone," he says. "I was scared to death. I spent the first two months sweating at night."

Rob says Al jumped in with both feet. "He never even checked to see if the water was cold or hot. He never even asked about pay."

In Al's opinion, the department's commitment to customer service was a joke. "We talked about the issues and how to fix them. Some guys had been beaten up so much in the past they wanted to quit, but they decided to give the new way a chance."

But other employees wanted no part of it. "They were some key players, but they didn't want to line up philosophically with the direction we were going," recalls Rob. "They were choosing not to be here. Knowing they'd produce a profit, I, as the owner, looked at Al and said, 'Are you sure?' Al pointed to our philosophy, mission, and values card. I said, 'OK, you're sure. Move on.'"

To replace those who left, Al hired several people who had never been service advisors before. He took people with high energy—positive people, customer-oriented people—and trained the necessary skills.

He also redesigned the service area. "We used to open the doors at 6:45 a.m. Two lanes, customers bumping into each other. It was like herding cattle." Al changed it to a single lane, with reservations every 15 minutes. "The goal was to give more personalized, quality time with the customer so the advisor can accurately report what the problem is."

In a few months, the service department's customer satisfaction scores soared in the top 10 percent in its region. Profits and market share rose significantly. Employee satisfaction made the biggest jump Rob had ever seen. "Before, we just fixed *cars*," Al says. "Now we realize that we're taking care of *people*."

"There are days when I'm down and I don't believe," Rob says. "Now Al comes and pumps me up, and I remember, Oh yeah! What we do *does* matter!"

MR. PERFECT

The first time Chuck Dery, the body shop manager, heard about the dealership's new philosophy, he told Rob it was BS. "I told him that a lot," he says. "There's no way a person can come in and tell me this fish story, and if we just do this, this is what will happen. I finally thought I'd try it, just to prove Rob wrong. But it backfired on me. Things kept getting better and better."

That's when Chuck became Mr. Perfect. "People would come up to me and say, 'How are you doing?' I'd say, 'Perfect.' They'd say, 'You can't be perfect.' Why wouldn't I be?

"If I let myself have a bad day, I'll go out and ruin every one of the guys in my department in about 10 seconds. Not a problem. If I come in with a grudge, or I had a fight with my wife, and let it affect me, I might as well take production and shut it down, because I'm the guy they look to.

"The quality of our work is the same as it always was. It was always good. The difference is attitude. If people are down, I coach 'em. Every situation's different. Maybe a guy has an argument with his wife and I'm the marriage counselor. I'm there for them and I get 120 percent back.

"When you're on the phone and somebody asks how you are, say 'Perfect.' I guarantee you people will call you on it. 'No, you can't be perfect.' I say every day is a perfect day. Feels better just sayin' it. I got 10 or 12 of my buddies saying it; it's all they say now. 'Perfect.'"

PLAYING YOUR PART

Julie Sweningson, parts manager, used to go to lunch with two service technicians. "All we did was complain about other people," she recalls.

Then one of the guys asked, "What do the other people say about me?"

Julie shook her head.

"No, come on," he said. "I can take it."

Julie told him, and it turned out he couldn't take it. "We stopped going to lunch after that."

Working in auto parts can be a thankless job. "You only hear the bad things if a part is back ordered and the customer is inconvenienced," she says. "People don't see everything you do to help them, locating parts, jumping through hoops."

But she stopped thinking about what she was getting and started focusing on what she was giving. "In the past, if a part was back ordered and we had quoted the customer a price, we'd just say you'll have to wait. Now if we quote a price, then find the part at another dealership, it's gonna cost us more and we don't make as much on it, but we get it anyway, to satisfy the customer. Short-term cost, long-term gain.

"You know, I don't understand how it works, but it does. The work is actually harder now, because we're busier. We have the same number of people cranking out the same number of parts, but we're enjoying it.

"I'd like to say I'm a lot different, but sometimes I slip back into that defensive mode. But I'm not as defensive. I'm calmer. Rob's shared a lot of ideas with us, and it's great to get that training. A raise wouldn't have helped my attitude at all. I've seen that done. You give a person a raise, but they still have a bad attitude. Here we are giving people the opportunity to change themselves, and that's better."

MAKING A DIFFERENCE

When Wayne Brueske's father owned a service station in Rochester, he rarely advertised. "He felt if he could not exist on word of mouth, he didn't deserve to be in business," says Wayne.

Growing up around cars, Wayne became a skilled mechanic. He joined Universal Ford in 1980. Like his father he was concerned about his customers, but by the late 1990s, he had begun to believe that management—under the fifth owner he had worked for—was not as concerned. "Everything was money, money, money."

Wayne didn't feel Universal cared much about its employees, either. Convincing management to buy tools and equipment that saved time—as well as the technicians' backs and knees—was a constant battle.

The battle wore on his attitude. One day he taped his employee number over the name on his shirt. "The service manager was really upset, but I figured I was just a number to them."

Wayne tried not to let his attitude affect his work, but it affected his outlook on almost everything else. He went to lunch with Julie Sweningson, complained, and walked around with his head down. "I was down in a hole so far I couldn't see light, much less touch it. It was to the point where either I left or I was gonna start having physical problems."

He had two other jobs lined up when Rob bought the dealership. When he heard Rob's initial talk, he said to himself, "Even if he does half of what he says, we'll be better off. Focusing on the customer was one of my values, and I thought, 'If I take another job, is it really going to change me? Or am I just taking my attitude to a different job?'"

Wayne stayed, but his attitude did not change overnight. When he and Rob had a run-in over one of Wayne's complaints—changing uniform companies—Rob said, "If it's so bad here, maybe you should move on."

It could have ended there, but both knew that would have been the easy way out. Rob offered to meet with Wayne and the other technicians every week. No other owner had ever made such an offer.

"At first I thought it was a chance to get some issues resolved in the shop," says Wayne. "It didn't turn out quite the way I envisioned it, but I guess I'm better off for the way it turned out. Mostly Rob talked about our values and how when we get outside of ourselves we can get around the other stuff."

Rob learned too. "I think getting inside their heads, them getting inside mine, seeing what I deal with and what they deal with, it helped us focus on what we had in common," he says.

"Before, I was probably scared to say what I really felt. Not knowing how it would be taken by management, I was afraid of losing my job," Wayne says. "But sitting down and talking with Rob, I feel we can talk about anything, without anything being held against each other."

Wayne chose to recapture something that he had hidden inside himself. "I started going out of my way, more than I used to, to make sure that people know I appreciate the little things they do to make my life easier or funnier or happier," he says. He joined an employee culture committee to find ways to recognize employees. One of their ideas was an appreciation card.

On the day the cards arrived at the dealership, Al Utesch decided to do something about some unruly shrubs on the south side of the showroom. Everyone had been complaining about how they looked. It was hot and sticky, but Al trimmed the shrubs. When he went into his office later, he discovered one of the cards. It said: *Thank you. You made a difference today*.

The card was from Wayne. "It may seem strange, a bunch of guys in a garage giving cards to each other, but it made my day," Al says.

Wayne knew that his journey would not always be smooth, and he knew that he, like others, would create bumps along the way. But now he had a vision of what his workplace *could* be.

In his spare time, Wayne volunteers with the Olmsted County Sheriff's Dive Team, searching ponds, lakes, and rivers for missing swimmers and evidence. One week they searched for a 13-year-old boy last seen at a swimming pond.

"We searched all day Saturday, but the water was really muddy and we called off the search at midnight," he recalls. "It was a terrible feeling. We searched Sunday. Nothing. Finally, on Monday, we found the body. All I could think about is how much I have to be thankful for. I've got a young son. I can still tuck him in tonight."

At a meeting with the service technicians that week, Rob talked about the dive team as a metaphor for work and life. "He said we don't swim around in murky water not knowing what we're going to find next because it's easy," Wayne says. "We do it because in the end we know that what we do every day makes a difference."

ONE DAY AT A TIME

By the spring of 2001, Rochester Ford Toyota was still early into its cultural journey. "A lot of people are on board, but it's a constant struggle," Brian Kopek says. "There are days when people call and tell us, 'You're no different than you were.' Swing and a miss. So we have to move forward with great patience, forgiveness, and understanding."

But the people of Rochester Ford Toyota had taken some important steps. In each of the five key areas of its philosophy—customer enthusiasm, employee satisfaction, financial performance, market effectiveness, and ongoing improvement—it had improved dramatically.

The dealership's "Have You Tried Our Fish?" billboard had been up for a year, and Rob—not unlike many leaders who shift from one "solution" to another—thought it was time to change it. "For me, FISH! had become a checkmark," he said. "It was like, OK, now our employees have a better sense of the journey. Let's check off the FISH! Philosophy. Done. Time to move on."

But when he suggested a new billboard, the managers looked at him like he was crazy. "Are you saying that as a culture, we truly understand the power of choosing our attitude?" they asked.

"No, not every day."

"And you believe that as a culture we are truly living in the present? We have no fear of the past, we don't fear the future, and we are always there for others?"

"Not always . . . not yet," Rob said.

"Do you think as a culture we completely understand the real energy that we will get in life from getting outside ourselves and truly helping other people?"

"Uhh . . . no."

"And you'd consider that this is an environment where play is a natural extension of a culture with high levels of trust and accountability?"

"No."

"And you are ready to move on?"

"Well, uh, no," Rob said. "I was . . . um, just saying if we ever did think about moving on . . ."

Rochester Ford Toyota finally did put up a new billboard. It read "Gone Fish" and it listed four points: "1. Play— Make It Fun; 2. Make Their Day— Go M.A.D. (Make a Difference); 3. Be There— Right Here, Right Now; and 4. Choose Your Attitude— Make Your Choice."

"They quickly pulled me back to staying the course. Discipline has never excited me. To live our vision, to live the FISH! Philosophy, is all about the art of discipline. I have faith in the values and in the people who are attracted to those values that we will always have more than we need. But I, being a human being and a skeptic, say, 'Well, sure, it's worked *so* far—but what *else* should we be doing?'

"There really is nothing else. We should continue to work on our vision and values every day."

SMALL BITES

YOU COULD BE NEXT

The Play Committee at one information systems department has come up with lots of fun activities. They've decorated the walls with butcher paper and invited employees to create their own graffiti (the only rule is no obscenities) and sponsored an Easter egg decorating contest and a name-the-baby-picture contest. But their most memorable stunt happens every few weeks, when one member of the department comes into her or his office to find that it has been decorated and she or he is the "Person of the Day." No one but the Play Committee knows who the next honoree will be.

What better way to remember the importance of making someone else's day than to have your colleagues make yours?

PAIN RELIEF FOR APRIL 15

How could you resist a tax preparation office that offers free aspirin? During tax season, the office does its best to give even customers who owe money a smile. All the staff members dress casually to keep out any "stiff" attitude. They give children lollipops and toys, and even dogs are welcome in the office. They also offer customers beer and wine to relieve their misery—it's just a joke, but it usually gets a laugh. This tiny office has just three tax preparers, and some office backup, but they complete over 2,000 returns in less than 10 weeks each spring.

"THE WHEELS ON THE BUS GO ROUND AND ROUND. . . ."

Remember riding the school bus as a kid? The driver often ignored you; you just hoped the bullies did too. Here's how the supervisor of safety and training for a large metropolitan school district in Colorado makes the ride fun and memorable.

Whenever he drives the school bus, he acknowledges every student that boards the bus. Randomly, as a student boards, he'll ask the student for his or her bus pass (his district doesn't use passes) just to get a reaction. When the kids respond that they don't have one, he says, "Well, you will just have to take a seat and have fun."

When the bus is almost full, he tells the kids to sing "Happy Birthday" to the next kid who gets on the bus. The reaction is always priceless. Sometimes he will ask a student with really cool shoes what size they are, and would she mind trading for the day?

The driver says the students enjoy this type of humor. He also is letting them know that he notices them and cares about them. He has had to discipline students much less often and they are having a lot more fun on their 77-passenger yellow limousine.

✂ **ANOTHER SCHOOL BUS DRIVER STORY!** ✂

A 140-employee company that provides school bus services has always had a policy of not allowing children at interviews. But one day the hiring director got a call from a woman who wanted to interview for a school bus driver job and needed to bring her two young children. The hiring director said, "I love kids! Bring them with you!" The interview went great and the applicant said, "Any company that loves children so much must be a good place to work." Recruitment and retention are two of the biggest challenges facing the bus industry; to meet that challenge, it takes people, like this hiring director, who are willing to bend the rules.

✂ **FLEECING THE CUSTOMER** ✂

Making someone's day is often about the element of surprise. At an optical store, an employee was visiting with a woman while her husband got his eyes examined. The woman mentioned that she spent much of her time sewing for her small grandchildren. "I used to sew for people all the time too," the employee said. "I have some Christmas sweatshirt fleece I'd love to give away." The customer thought it sounded great but couldn't believe she was serious. But within a few days, the customer had received the free fleece in the mail.

❧ A SMALL RED RIBBON ❧

In the days following the horror of September 11, 2001, it was pretty quiet in most workplaces. Many people, especially those of us who live far from New York or Washington, D.C., wondered, "What can *I* do to help?" So we donated money. We gave blood.

The day after the attacks, P.J., one of our colleagues, went to a fast-food restaurant. She was greeted by the manager, who was holding a spool of red ribbon. The woman cut a small piece of ribbon and asked P.J. if it was OK to pin it on her. P.J. watched the manager pin ribbons on dozens of people—office workers, high school students, construction workers. For a moment, people who ordinarily would have dashed in and out, barely acknowledging one another, were connected.

❧ CODE "SWIM" ❧

Remember the hospital where fun is one of its core values? When a patient is discharged, a Code Swim is called—meaning the patient is "swimming" away. The staff gathers in the hall and gives them a grand send-off, complete with hugs and, almost always, tears.

❧ LET THEM EAT CAKE ❧

Harry Paul has a son who plays baseball. At the end of the season it is customary to provide treats for the team. His wife,

Mary, prepared a delicious chocolate sheet cake with a thick chocolate frosting and Harry was drafted to deliver the cake, paper plates, napkins, and plastic utensils.

As the game ended and the sweaty players assembled in their soiled uniforms for a treat, Harry looked at them and then at the paper plates he was holding. On the spur of the moment he said, "We can cut this cake in little squares and serve it with napkins—or we can just dive in."

The players said, "We would like it on plates with plastic forks and napkins, Mr. Paul. Not!"

Twelve pairs of hands reached for heaping handfuls of cake. As Harry picked up the pieces, the startled coach was being chased around the baseball diamond by 11 boys and one girl wanting to share their good fortune.

Section Three—BE THERE

You can multi-task with "stuff," but you need to "be there" for people.

At Pike Place Fish the fishmongers have learned that customers want your full attention when you are with them. A big part of their magic is being fully present.

How much do you actually get done when you are in one place thinking about a different place? Why not commit to being in one place at a time? When you are present—not dwelling on what happened in the past or worried about what may happen in the future—you are fully attuned to opportunities that develop and to the needs of the people you encounter. You gain a healthier perspective and the capacity for greater focus and creativity.

In no line of work is "being there" more important than in health care. When you try to provide the best possible patient care while simultaneously attempting to reduce costs and deal with constant change, a stressful workplace can be the consequence. That's why this field offers important lessons for all industries and situations.

"Be There" means be present—fully present—*especially* when you are interacting with another person. If that person happens to be vulnerable, your ability to be present can have both positive and healing effects. Patients in hospitals and clinics, residents of nursing homes, those living in homes for the developmentally disabled, and children all share a high level of vulnerability. The capacity of caregivers to "be there" for the people they serve is perhaps the single most powerful quality-of-care variable. If you doubt that for a second, simply remember how you felt the last time someone gave you her or his undivided attention.

DAD

A few years ago my dad had a massive stroke. He lives in a nursing home now. While he needs total care and can't speak in a way that is understandable, he understands everything and is quite verbal.

It is hard to staff nursing homes. The work can be unpleasant and depressing, and the pay marginal. Hence the nursing homes in the Minneapolis area are often the first place of employment for new workers who come to town. At the home where Dad resides this is certainly the case. One day a new aide came into Dad's room to get him ready for the day. As she proceeded to get Dad dressed and toileted, she conversed with him in a way that made him the center of her universe. The fact that he could not be understood didn't seem to

bother her as she went about her job. You could see his counte-
nance lighten as she spoke with him.

I have seen others come into Dad's room, often wearing
white uniforms, and I have watched them continue to talk
with their colleagues in the hall as they went about their routine tasks. I could literally see Dad tense up. According to his
record, at times like this he actually says a word or two that is
quite clear.

Unconsciously these staff members treated Dad as if he
were a person who had only physical needs—and they performed required tasks with him and nothing more. The new
minimum-wage aide performed her tasks equally well. But
she acted with a wisdom that took into consideration that Dad
has a soul and spirit also, and she nurtured these by *who* she
was *being* while she went about her work.

"I DON'T HAVE TIME!"

Carr Hagerman, a gifted speaker who works at Chart-
House Learning, was talking with a group of nurses when one
of them loudly proclaimed she did not have time for all this
stuff. She said she was too busy already. But another nurse immediately said, "I don't think we are talking about doing anything extra. I think this is about *who* we are being while we are
doing the things we need to do anyway. When we are with a
patient we can be *physically* present or we can be *fully* present.
The difference to the patient is considerable. How much of the

stuff we are distracted by as we work with a patient actually gets done anyway? So why not be fully present while we are doing the things we have to do anyway?"

The nurses sat in silence pondering the wisdom of their colleague then launched into a high-energy discussion about being there for patients—physically, emotionally, and spiritually—and how that is their tradition as nurses.

What follows is the story of a remarkable group of health care professionals who have transformed a part of the hospital system in which they work by devoting themselves to the idea of being there for their patients and for each other.

The Gift of Being Present:
Missouri Baptist Medical Center

Shari Bommarito, R.N., became a nurse because she wanted to be there for the whole person—emotionally *and* physically. "I once cared for a patient whose cancer was terminal," she says. "His wife could not stand to see him suffer and wanted to turn the ventilator off, but didn't want him to know. He wanted to turn the ventilator off, but thought he needed to keep fighting for his wife's sake.

"I had enough time back then on my shift to talk to them and figure this out. I sat them down together and I said, 'You should tell each other how you really feel.' They were holding hands when I closed the curtain. Finally she came out and said, 'He is ready to die.'"

Sometimes nursing is about profound moments, and sometimes it is about pills and bedpans, but it is *always* about being there for people who need you.

But while medical care has improved dramatically from a technical standpoint and nurses are better trained, there are fewer opportunities to be there for people's emotional needs. Spending time with the patient has been replaced by the need to spend time monitoring technology. Hospital stays are shorter and the list of tasks that must be completed during that time is longer.

"Holding hands comes last on the list," Shari said. "If you get to it, great, but if you don't, that's the way it is."

"I HATE THIS"

On a sweltering summer day in 1999, Shari sat in her daily traffic jam. Her knuckles were white. She had a headache. She was recently divorced, one of her children had just been diagnosed with asthma, and she was working full-time again. Being away from her kids made the hour's drive to work every day even more frustrating. "I hate this," she said to herself, and suddenly the words, "Missouri Baptist" came into her mind.

At the time, Shari was a clinical nurse educator at Barnes-Jewish Hospital in St. Louis, Missouri. Barnes-Jewish is one of the best hospitals in the country (*U.S. News & World Report* ranked it seventh in 2000) and the anchor of BJC HealthCare, the area's largest health system. "It's high tech and high speed," Shari explains. "You see things happening there you don't see in other hospitals."

Missouri Baptist Medical Center, located in western St. Louis County, had recently joined BJC HealthCare. It was much smaller than Barnes-Jewish, though its cancer, heart, and orthopedics centers were highly regarded, and the number of births at the hospital would quadruple over the next two years. Missouri Baptist was also located five minutes from Shari's home.

Despite her doubts about leaving Barnes-Jewish—to Shari it seemed like the center of the world—she interviewed at Missouri Baptist and was hired as a clinical nurse educator. Her job: to make sure the nursing staff had the resources they needed to remain clinically competent.

She came to work her first day "scared to death," but during her tour, almost everyone she passed smiled, made eye contact, and said hello. Shari was a little uncomfortable at first. At Barnes-Jewish the half-mile-long hallways teemed with people on the run, and there never seemed to be enough time to greet people.

"These people are almost *too* nice," she said to her guide with a laugh.

"That is an expectation," the guide said. "You stop to help people when they are lost, say hello to people, smile, just be friendly."

"Wow, I can do this," Shari thought. Then, at lunch, a nurse asked her where she would be working.

"Fifth floor neuro-renal."

"Oh my, you have *that* floor?" the nurse said.

Shari's nervousness returned. "No one says something like that to you on your first day," she thought. "What have I walked into?"

After lunch Shari went up to the fifth floor. She was greeted warmly by the unit's head nurse, Hilda VanNatta, R.N.

She took Shari's hands in hers. "I am glad you are here." Shari nodded. "Hilda looks tired," she thought to herself.

FEELING THE PRESSURE

Missouri Baptist has always had a reputation for having a compassionate nursing staff. "I have always had caring people on this floor," Hilda says. "One Thanksgiving, when two of my staff got off work, they brought a special dinner to a woman who had no family, and gave up their own evening to spend the holiday with her."

But even caring people can feel the pressure of working on a floor like neuro-renal. "We take care of people with strokes, multiple sclerosis, brain tumors, seizures. Some have had surgery," explains Hilda. "The renal patients are complicated because their kidney failure has caused so many other problems. Many come to us every six weeks or so for dialysis; they're known as the 'Frequent Flyers.'"

"A few years ago many of these patients would have been in intensive care," says Cathy Flora, R.N., neuro-renal clinical nurse manager. "Now our staff's technical skills are a lot higher and we have the technology to care for them on this floor."

Nearly all of the patients on neuro-renal are so ill and weak they can't sit or stand on their own. It takes two or three nurses to lift, move, and bathe them, even to feed them. "Because some patients are in isolation rooms, every time you go in you have to put on a gown and mask," Shari said. "Once you are in, if you need something, you need another nurse to bring it to you, or you have to take everything off, get what you need, then put it all back on again. So you rely on others a lot."

In the fall of 1999, the number of tasks was growing and time seemed to be shrinking. "The mindset was, 'I get my tasks done before I help anybody else,'" Shari says. "I would see people standing in the halls with gowns on, looking for people to help them. When people did help each other, they weren't acknowledging or thanking each other. The thought was, 'You're doing your job. Why should I thank you?'"

Sharon Sanders, R.N., who had recently become a nurse, knew that her coworkers were caring people. "I didn't think people were always helpful or supportive of each other," she says. "People were focusing on the negative side of every-thing—not always—but I was pretty discouraged coming on the floor sometimes. Then again, being a new nurse, I thought, 'I guess this is what the real world is like.'"

A "FISHY" INVITATION

Hilda and Cathy agreed that their staff desperately needed help with teamwork. Before planning the training, Shari Bommarito asked the staff how they felt they were performing in six areas: teamwork, positive team attitude, communication, support for others, satisfaction working within the team, and having a say within the team.

Just 30 percent felt a strong presence of teamwork. Only a third of the staff felt strongly that there was good communica-tion among team members, and just 25 percent felt strongly that there was support for team members, a positive team attitude, and satisfaction working within the team. Only 15 percent felt strongly that they had a say within their team.

In other words, only 15 to 30 percent of the staff really liked their jobs. Hilda was willing to consider almost any solution. Shari suggested an unlikely one—the FISH! Philosophy, which she learned about at Barnes-Jewish Hospital. "We needed teamwork, and the only thing I knew for certain was that it was about teamwork," Shari says.

Shari created flyers with a picture of a fish dressed like a clown, juggling stars, clams, and crabs, and the words, "There's Something Fishy Going On Here . . ." She posted the flyers throughout the floor, giving people a few days to wonder what in the heck this was about. Then she invited everyone who worked on the floor—nurses, nurse assistants, doctors, housekeepers—to learn about the FISH! Philosophy. Most important, she mentioned she would be serving homemade cheesecake.

They came in groups of 10, usually just before their shifts or after. Shari showed a tape of the fishmongers. She explained that what they do every day—staying present and attuned to people's needs, doing something special for people, taking responsibility for their attitude even on the toughest days, and finding ways to enjoy their day—is what being a nurse is all about.

She pointed to Justin, a young fishmonger, who, when asked about his positive attitude, said: "It's a simple choice."

"Did you hear what he said?" Shari asked. "He's a 24-year-old kid and he's *choosing* to make a difference in the lives of people who are buying fish! If he can do it, we can choose to make a difference in the lives of people who are sick and dying."

Then Shari told about her drive to and from work. It was construction season, lanes were torn up, and the traffic was so busy it was almost impossible to get onto the road. "On the way home I stop at every gas station and let people pull onto the road in front of me. They wave and their kids blow kisses at me. I'm happy for them because I understand what it's like to wait.

"That's the idea. Take time to be there for people. Do something nice for someone else. When they say thank you, it feels so good you will want to find someone else to help."

Not everyone was convinced. One nurse, sure that this was another "program" designed to drain more effort out of the staff, said, "What do they want from us now?"

"*They* don't want anything," Shari responded. "*They* want you to enjoy what you're doing for others. *They* want you to have fun. *They* want you to stay. What do *you* want?"

The nurse was silent. "I want the same thing," she finally said.

THE GREAT FISH GIVEAWAY

At the end of each class, Shari gave each person a small plastic fish. She had found them in a novelty catalog and cut a slit in each fish's tail so it fit on employee badges.

"When someone does something nice for you, give them

your fish," she told the staff. "If you need more fish, I have plenty."

Before long, the staff was handing out fish everywhere. When people were overwhelmed, their coworkers started saying, "Let me do this treatment for you." Housekeepers helped nurses feed patients when no one else was available. People did favors for others on their breaks. "We started feeling like a team working together instead of everybody doing their own thing," Cathy said.

When Shari went to the cafeteria one day, she saw that the cashier was wearing a fish. "I don't know what it's for, but a nurse gave it to me," the cashier said. "She said I was being nice."

"Now you can give it to someone who does something nice for you," Shari said.

The cashier nodded in understanding. "Yep," she said.

According to Sharon Sanders, the plastic fish was an ice-breaker. "Sometimes adults have a hard time saying, 'You did a good job,' or 'I appreciate what you did for me,'" she says. "We hadn't been saying that to each other. Now we were."

The fish also gave real-time feedback. "Nurses are task-oriented," explains Cathy. "They want and need to hear specific praise for specific things."

If some people initially helped others because they wanted a plastic fish, the real reward soon became apparent. "Making someone's day is not just being pleasant," Shari Bommarito says. "It's about going out of your way to do something for another person. It's like an endorphin; it feels so good, you want to do more."

And in the process, the staff learned things they never knew about each other. "One of our secretaries kind of intimidated me," Shari said. "But I was so wrong about her. She would go out of her way to do anything for anyone. People started giving her fish and she started collecting them. She hooked her fish together and soon she had a chain of fish a foot-and-a-half long."

PLAYING WHILE SICK

The nurses also gave plastic fish to their patients. "If patients were a little crabby, I'd give them a fish and say, 'Here's a friend to keep you happy,'" Sharon Sanders said. "One man had a string of seven or eight little fish, and they accidentally got thrown in the laundry. He was pretty upset, and we replaced his fish in a hurry."

Carol Johnson, R.N., gave a fish to a patient who had made an extraordinary effort in his therapy that day. "He acted like I had given him a million dollars," she says.

Even some unlikely patients responded. "We had a dialysis patient who was extremely depressed," Cathy says. "That's a problem for many of our patients, but this woman was young and she had kids at home. She had a lot to live for and she was about to give up. She just lay in bed and did nothing.

"Hilda and I started giving her fish to get her to participate in her treatment. First we gave her plastic fish, then stuffed fish. Soon she started getting out of bed and began to progress on her own, and she started asking for fish when she did. I can't say what turned her around, but the fish were part of it. She really talked about her fish and showed them to people who came by."

At the same time, Shari Bommarito began noticing more nurses spending more time sitting with patients. "Usually you'd go in with a clipboard and stand over them," she says. "But I saw them sitting so they could get down to the patient's eye level. That little thing meant a lot, especially to our older patients."

Many patients began asking for fish, so they could give them to staff when they were extra nice or helpful. Some patients and family members wrote thank-you notes to the nurses on fish stationery.

And before anyone realized it, people on a floor full of sick and dying patients were smiling and playing with one another. "I'm playful—that's just me—so I just brought it to work with me," Sharon Sanders says. "Before, I hadn't been comfortable with that side of myself in the workplace. I didn't know it was acceptable to act that way. But I think we should try to make people's lives happy, whether it's in the middle of their life or the end."

She understands how important that is. Several years ago, her husband, Scot, was diagnosed with leukemia. At the time they had three small children. After having been a stay-at-home mom for several years, Sharon became a nurse. "I've had to deal with a lot of hard things, but you have got to live each day to the fullest and be the happiest that you can every day," she says. "I can't imagine living any other way."

COMPETING FOR STICKERS

Shari Bommarito returned from a two-week vacation in January 2000. When she came off the elevator on the fifth floor, all she could see were fish. There were fish hanging from the ceiling, fish magnets in patient rooms, and a poster on the wall that said FISH TEAMS.

"I'm walking down the hall wondering what happened," she says. "When I open the door to Hilda and Cathy's office, they're giggling! They had been talking about how to prepare for a visit from representatives of the Joint Commission on Accreditation of Health Care Organizations."

"We had about 200 items on a checklist, and I wasn't sure how to do it," Hilda explains. "One morning I was reading the Bible about Moses and how he didn't know how he was going to get everything done to get the Israelites to the Promised Land. His father-in-law, Jethro, said you need to form teams and get everyone involved. That gave me an idea."

Hilda and Cathy organized several teams. Each team had eight or nine people, including one physician. Each team appointed captains and named itself after a fish. Names included Barracudas, Purple Tangs, Angelfish, Piranhas, and Night Groupers.

Hilda and Cathy issued a friendly challenge. Teams whose members completed certain tasks, such as finishing their self-study packets for accreditation, would receive stickers. At the end of three months, the team with the most stickers would get a party and prizes.

To help the teams learn what they needed to, Hilda and Cathy created contests. One featured fish-shaped pieces of paper with questions about various aspects of patient care. When staff members wrote the answer on the bottom of the paper, their team got points for stickers. Teams competed to make posters to help educate coworkers on infrequently prescribed medications. As teams accumulated stickers, they also accumulated knowledge that would help them provide better, more efficient patient care.

"The fish teams found a lot of ways to improve," Shari said. "One of our physicians complained that his patients' blood sugar [levels] weren't always being documented in the right place on the chart, and when they weren't he had to go hunting for it. One of the teams asked the doctor if they could use his picture. He was a good sport. They superimposed his head on a cartoon picture of King Neptune and printed on it, *Please Document Your Blood Sugars!* They posted copies everywhere on the floor. The nurses laughed, but they also started documenting blood sugars correctly."

In the process, play boosted productivity. "We really wanted those stickers," Sharon Sanders says. "We were like little kids. We would stand at the chart and say to each other, 'Look, my team has seven stickers and yours only has four.'"

THE CLARINET AND THE CONDUCTOR

When Leo Carter, a nurse's assistant, learned about the new philosophy on neuro-renal, it brought a big smile to his face. "I said, 'This is what we need. We just needed to put a name to it.'"

A few years earlier, when Leo was 22, his father had died. "It was all very mysterious to me," he says. "I wish I had known half the things I know now. But there was no one who ever came to me and tried to take that pain away.

"When I got the chance to work at Missouri Baptist and had that first experience with working with someone who was in pain, and got to do something about it, I knew then I could never turn back. I used to work with cancer patients and I had to learn that for some of them, life really is short. Why make that time full of memories of pain, when you can try to throw some joy to them?"

Leo decided to create joy with music. "When patients are down, I sing little songs to them, or I do my own little Elvis impression, and it perks them up. Recently we had an older patient who wouldn't eat. Her daughter came to get me because she said I seemed to have a way with her mother. I sat down with the patient and said I would sing a little for her if she would take a few bites. She ate half her meal. That was pretty cool.

"I really enjoy getting a rapport going with the patient like that, and getting a comfort level with their family members. Nothing makes me feel better than when a family member tells me, 'Knowing that you're going to be here tonight will let me sleep with ease.'"

But for many neuro-renal patients, sleeping peacefully isn't easy. "We call them 'sundowners,'" Leo says. "When the sun goes down, some people who seem mentally clear and are easy to deal with during the day seem to lose their sense of place. They may become confused and agitated. They don't know where they are and they don't know who you are."

Sometimes the sundowners try to get out of bed. "Occasionally we put people in a chair and wheel them to the nurses' station for a while," Leo says. "We tell them it's so they can keep us company, but it's really so we can keep an eye on them so they don't fall."

One night Leo was taking vital signs from a patient who was in his 90s and near death. The patient was incoherent, agitated, and trying to pull out his IV. Leo tried to calm him down, but nothing was working. So he started singing softly. That didn't work either. Leo began to think he might have to get a doctor's order to restrain the man. He never liked having to do that.

Just then Olya Senchenkova, R.N., came into the room. As she and Leo considered what to do next, Olya said, "Did you know he used to be the conductor of a symphony orchestra?"

"Really?" Leo said. He had a long list of duties yet to complete, but he thought for a moment. "You know, I have my clarinet in my car."

"Go get it," she said. "I'll cover for you."

Leo had played clarinet in his college's marching band; his niece had been borrowing the clarinet and had just returned it. He assembled the instrument, then practiced for a minute or two. "I hadn't played in a year," Leo says. "I didn't want this master conductor to rip it out of my mouth."

Leo returned to the room. He played the first classical piece that came to mind, "Peter and the Wolf," and then the theme from *The Muppet Show*.

As the soft, mellow notes drifted through the room, something happened. The old man stopped thrashing. He closed his eyes and smiled. Lying on his back, he raised his arms and began to wave them back and forth. Perhaps, deep in his mind, he was standing in a great concert hall once again, wearing coat and tails, with a baton in his strong hands, leading *his* orchestra. After a few minutes the old man's arms dropped slowly to his sides and he slept quietly through the night.

It was the only night Leo took care of the conductor. Leo had the next few days off and when he returned to work, he learned that the man had died. The conductor's family said he was peaceful when he left them, and they were thankful for that.

LETTING WONDERFUL EMERGE

In May 2000, several months after introducing the FISH! Philosophy to neuro-renal, Shari Bommarito repeated her original teamwork survey. The turnaround, especially in the number of staff who *strongly* felt the presence of teamwork, was remarkable.

	SEPTEMBER 1999	**MAY 2000**
FELT INDICATOR WAS	TEAMWORK	TEAMWORK
LACKING	25	10
PRESENT	45	15
STRONG	30	75

FELT INDICATOR WAS	ATTITUDE	ATTITUDE
LACKING	25	15
PRESENT	50	10
STRONG	25	75

FELT INDICATOR WAS	COMMUNICATION	COMMUNICATION
LACKING	15	20
PRESENT	52	15
STRONG	33	65

FELT INDICATOR WAS	SUPPORT	SUPPORT
LACKING	25	10
PRESENT	50	15
STRONG	25	75

FELT INDICATOR WAS	SATISFACTION	SATISFACTION
LACKING	25	15
PRESENT	50	10
STRONG	25	75

FELT INDICATOR WAS	HAVE A SAY	HAVE A SAY
LACKING	33	20
PRESENT	52	15
STRONG	15	65

"In the first survey, when I asked them what a team was, people said the names of sports teams, like the Rams or Cardinals," Shari says. "Now they said *their* teams—the Barracuda, the Angelfish.

"And instead of saying, 'I don't have time to help you,' people said, 'I'm busy right now, but I'll be there in a second. Can you wait?' That's what was missing. Those wonderful people were there all the time. They just didn't have time to be wonderful because they weren't working together.

"The nurses had stopped being nurses. All we did was say, 'This is why you came here. Have fun. Take a few minutes to be there for your patient. We will work as a team. We will get the job done together.'

"That's what Leo did. He had a list of tasks as long as anyone, but he took a few minutes to play the clarinet for a confused old man. He was able to do that because Olya watched his patients. They worked as a team.

"And instead of sitting in my office listening to people in the halls say, 'I need help!' now I got off my rear to go help them. I had to walk the talk, too."

SPREADING THE JOY

Word of what was happening on the neuro-renal floor spread throughout Missouri Baptist. "You'd get on the elevator with your fish on your badge and people would say, 'Hey, you're from the fish floor,'" Leo says.

The neuro-renal staff won Missouri Baptist's annual Quality Team Award, given to the team that did the most to improve patient care. As part of the award, the staff won $1,000. They gave half to the family of one of their patients for a Christmas present and used the rest for a Christmas party.

"Patients and relatives often told us they could see that what we were doing really helped patients," says Lois Wright, R.N., director of nursing services.

Soon other floors began asking for the FISH! Philosophy. "Our floor had a hard time with that," Shari says. "We kind of wanted it for ourselves. But then we said, 'How fishy is that?'" Soon they were sharing what they had discovered.

But when some operating room staff asked Shari to teach them about the philosophy, she hesitated. High stress, a staffing shortage, and resistance to change had fueled a deep sense of negativity there. Just as she had feared, during her presentation some people sat in the back and said things like, "Keep your fish. Give us the cash."

Such comments didn't stop others from trying to bring some positive energy to the OR. The staff created a bulletin board where you could recognize coworkers who went out of their way to help someone, and Nancy Hesselbach, R.N., director of surgical services, bought a talking fish to hang on the wall.

Then somebody stole the fish.

Upset, Nancy posted a note asking the kidnappers to return her fish or leave money to replace him. The kidnappers responded by leaving a message on Hesselbach's answering machine: "We have Billy. Do what we say or you'll never see him again." In the background, Billy was gurgling.

Nancy made up a flyer saying, "Please Return My Baby Billy," and offered a prize for information leading to the arrest and conviction of his kidnappers. His captors responded by dropping a can of tuna on her desk and a note saying this is what was to become of her beloved Billy.

"The staff were really into what was happening to Billy," Nancy says. "They wrote poems, songs, and epitaphs to Billy. We outlined the shape of a fish on our floor with masking tape and set it up like a crime scene with a 'Do Not Cross' police line. People were in stitches over this for weeks."

Before anyone realized it, the OR staff—including those most negative about the FISH! Philosophy—were having fun at work.

The "kidnappers" finally instructed Nancy to bring coffee and donuts to the next staff meeting. She complied, and later found a talking fish resembling Billy with duct tape over his mouth. "Billy's back and he'll never be the same. He's better than ever. Thanks for a successful campaign," read the accompanying note.

The OR later organized committees to explore ways to create a better workplace environment. "There are still people who want nothing to do with it, but others are trying to make a difference," says Shari. "They are making baby steps."

Missouri Baptist began to spread the FISH! Philosophy to other areas of the medical center. "Every hospital system in our state is having trouble recruiting nurses," explains Sheila Reed, a program development specialist at the Clinical Nursing Institute. "Instead of just trying to recruit, we need to retain our excellent staff. Money makes some difference, but the underlying reason most people like their jobs is due to other factors, such as their coworkers or the atmosphere."

As of summer 2001, Admitting was the latest area to introduce these principles. "The last time I walked down there, they had fish on the top of their computers," Shari says. "I said, 'You're right on target.' That's why we decorated our area with fish. Patients and visitors will ask about it and your staff are going to have to reaffirm it, and every time they talk about it, they're going to start walking it. You just have to keep cheering for them."

SWIMMING IN THE SAME DIRECTION

Back on neuro-renal, the work didn't change. It was still just as tiring, frustrating, and emotionally draining. What did change was the attitude the staff chose to bring to their work.

"We had a patient with renal failure who was with us for several weeks," Shari says. "Her family was nice but very demanding. At times it seemed like her husband expected more care and more time than any nurse could have given. The nurses worked hard to fulfill his high expectations and it didn't seem like it was ever really enough."

"We had been through a lot with this family and, yeah, they had frustrated all of us at some point, but they were frustrated too," Sharon Sanders says. "They were watching their loved one die and we had to realize where they were at."

On the day the woman was to be discharged, Shari Bommarito was working in her office when Hilda stuck her head in. "Come out here right now," Hilda said.

In the hall was the patient's husband. A group of nurses was gathered around him. He was holding a watercolor painting.

"I painted this years ago and it never sold," he said. "I'm not sure why." He held up the painting for the nurses. Swimming on the canvas were beautiful tropical fish of many colors.

"My painting is called *Harmony*," he said. "Like the fish in this painting, you are all different. You are different people and different colors and you come from different places . . . but you are all swimming in the same direction. You made a difference for my wife . . . and I would like you to have this painting."

Shari stood in the back of the crowd, stunned. "This is one of those moments you hold on to," she says. "Hilda and I are sobbing, and I look at these nurses and I'm thinking, 'Do you hear what he's saying to you? Do you realize what you've done? You made a difference! You didn't think it was enough, but it made a difference!'"

"A SIMPLE CHOICE"

As recognition for being the first floor at Missouri Baptist to introduce the FISH! Philosophy, the staff was awarded bright purple-and-blue jackets decorated with tropical fish. No other floor can wear them.

In the process, Shari realized something essential about the FISH! Philosophy. "When we started all this, I worshiped the guys at Pike Place Fish. They're wonderful. But they're no different than we are."

Pike Place Fish has fans known as the Yogurt Dudes, who come during their lunch hour just to watch the fishmongers work. "Leo took pictures of the staff, cut them out in the shape of a fish, and put them on a poster," Shari says. "Pretty soon patients wanted their picture on the poster too. We said, 'Oh my gosh, we have Yogurt Dudes!'

"Then I heard one of our nurses telling a graduate nurse she was training, 'You have to choose to be here and you have to *choose* whether you want to have a good day or not. It's a simple choice.'

"I walked by her a few minutes later and I told her, 'You are a fishmonger.'"

SMALL BITES

✄ ROBBIE'S STORY ✄

We heard this story from a blood transfusion service. Every week since birth, a four-year-old boy named Robbie needed all of his blood replaced. Every month Robbie's parents went to one of the service's seven locations and thanked every worker, volunteer, and donor for making it possible for their son to live. Many employees kept a picture of Robbie in their offices to remind them of who they were "being" while serving others. Is there something *you* can bring to work to remind *you* to "be there?"

✄ TWO HUNDRED COOKIES ✄

A friend named Harry stopped at a fast-food restaurant and placed an order that included a cookie. The server said, "And would you like a cookie with that today?" The next time Harry returned to the restaurant, he placed the same order, cookie included, with a different server. Again, the server politely asked, "Would you like a cookie with that?"

The third time Harry dealt with yet another server. This

time he was feeling a little mischievous. He placed his order, then added, "And I would like two hundred cookies." To which the server said, without a trace of irony, "I'll get that for you, sir. And would you like a cookie with that?"

Yes, the employees were told to say that. But were they really present when they did?

✄ LOOKING FOR BLUSH ✄

When an elderly woman came into an optical store looking for blush, it would have been easy for the store employee just to point her in the direction of the cosmetics store. But she took time off to walk her through the mall to the store, then out to her car. The elderly woman said just three words but they came straight from her heart: "God bless you."

✄ SITTING WITH MOM ✄

In December 2000, Steve's 84-year-old mom moved in with him and his wife. They took the family room with attached bathroom on the first floor and made it her home. "It has been delightful to be able to knock on the door and drop in," he says. "I haven't had this proximity to Mom since I was a kid."

The example set by the fish guys has helped Steve "be there" for his mother. At first he would knock on her door and go in and chat while standing. Something didn't feel quite right but it took a while to understand what was missing. Now he knocks, goes in, and sits on the couch. The act of sitting down helps him to be there and makes the visit more pleasant for both of them—

even if it is a short stay. Sitting not only sends a message to his mom but it also serves as a cue for him to be where he is.

Recently Steve noticed something his mother does to "be there" for him: "When I visit Mom and she has the TV on, she picks up a pencil to push the remote and turn off the TV, something she can't do with her fingers. This gesture speaks volumes about how she values my visits. Why didn't I notice that before?"

🐟 **THANKS FOR MAKING A DIFFERENCE** 🐟

After John Christensen had given a speech, five or six people at a time came up to him to talk more about how they could bring more energy to their work. "I tried to listen to them all," he recalls. "One woman was so excited about all the things she was doing at work. I heard what she was saying and I said, 'That's lovely,' but I didn't really look her in the eye."

Two days later John remembered the encounter. She had given him her card. He immediately called her, apologized for not being present, and thanked her for everything she was doing to improve the lives of her coworkers. A few days later, he got a letter from her. "You called me at an incredible time," she wrote. "I thought I wasn't making a difference anymore. Now I know I do."

🐟 **WHAT IS LOVE?** 🐟

The other day Steve Lundin was sitting at his desk and daydreaming while looking at a picture of his daughter Melissa, her husband Paul, and their two darling children. "I am really proud of the way Missy and Paul are raising their children and Mia and Madeleine are thriving," Steve says. "I thought about all the love that is present in their home. When the word love came to mind I asked myself a question. 'What is love?' The answer followed quickly. 'Love, for a child, is being there.'"

⚝ GOING DOG-FISHING ⚝

Paul, a university dean, had by his own admission become a workaholic. But one day, hearing about how the fishmongers practice being present, he decided to be there for himself and those he loved. He visualized the most important person in his life, Joyce, and a dog walking on the shores of a lake.

That afternoon, to the amazement of his colleagues and his family, he left work on time for the first time in months. And that afternoon Paul and Joyce walked their dog along Lake Superior. The rest of the summer, he left work no later than 5 p.m. He and Joyce often walked—and he and his dog often went dog-fishing (retrieving tennis balls from the lake).

⚝ A VALUABLE SERVICE ⚝

We expect the people who serve us in stores and restaurants to be there for us. *But are we there for them?* Our colleague Carr Hagerman was talking on his cell phone as a clerk rang up his purchases. Suddenly, he said into the cell phone, "I need to hang up now so I can be with the clerk."

The clerk looked into Carr's eyes. "Thank you," she said. "You just made me valuable."

Section Four—CHOOSE YOUR ATTITUDE

The attitude you have right now is the one you are choosing.
Is it the one you want?

From our very first visit to Pike Place Fish, we were struck by the number of conversations about choice. The fish guys are always talking about their choice to be at work and their choice to have a good day. I can only speculate about where the idea emerged. A few of the guys are 12-steppers like me, and choice is certainly a part of that process. "Choose your attitude" provides a solid base for this marvelous business culture.

THE SNAKE STORY

I first heard the following story at a Stephen Covey seminar in 1985. I know the story has been around longer than that, but it was the first time I heard it.

Three high school graduates, two men and a woman, were walking in the Arizona desert when a rattlesnake, coiled in the dark, bit the woman. The two guys took off after the snake and eventually caught it and brought it back. Meanwhile the woman, left to deal with the venom, nearly died.

The point is that at one time or another, life bites us all. The choice is the same in each case. We can chase the snakes in our lives or deal with the poison.

In the story that follows, a roofing company demonstrates in many ways the power of choice. I especially love their willingness to enter into what can be difficult conversations. As a result they are proving the truth of the following statement:

> The greatest discovery of my generation is that a human being can alter his life by altering his attitude.
>
> —William James (1842–1910)

Let It Rain:
Tile Technology Roofing Company

It's warm inside the truck, and the coffee's hot, but every squeak of the windshield wipers betrays the morning's cold reality. Rain is pouring from the gray, mountain-lined skies of Tacoma, and it's just a few degrees from turning into snow.

There's a Catch-22 in roofing: You wear rain gear to stay dry, but lifting thousands of pounds of tile shingles all day makes you sweat, and then you're freezing *and* wet 20 feet in the air.

Russ Vieselmeyer would rather be sitting in front of a blazing fire thinking about snowboarding, but he and his crew from Tile Technology Roofing Company have a job to finish. When they put the last piece of tile in place later today, rain won't penetrate this family's home for several decades.

As Russ piles out of the truck, he knows he has a choice today. He gives one of his crew a high-five and as the freezing drops sting his face he stares up into the heavens and laughs.

"Is that all you got?" he yells. "Bring it on!"

CHOOSING TO BE GREAT

Lives are made up of millions of choices. Some are made for you but it's the choices you make that count the most.

Doug Vieselmeyer, Russ's older brother, was seven when his parents divorced. Then, his mother, Connie, was stricken with lupus, which can cause the immune system to attack healthy tissues and organs. She was 6′ 1″ and strong, but the disease—which was initially misdiagnosed—left her so weak she couldn't even open baby food jars for Doug's younger siblings. "I would run over and ask the neighbor lady to do it," Doug recalls.

Lupus often comes and goes without warning. Sometimes Connie Vieselmeyer spent long stretches where she was nearly bedridden. Sometimes the disease went into remission. "She went back to college, finished her teaching degree, and taught third grade for a few years," Doug says. "Then the lupus came back."

While some days were better than others, "she still found joy in every day of her life. There was always love in our house. If she could no longer do something physically, she focused on what she *could* do. When all she could do was sit, she made gifts for people, because she couldn't afford to buy them."

Because of his mother's illness, Doug had to grow up quickly. "I kind of missed my childhood, parts of it anyway," he explains. "We were on welfare, and kids will humiliate you any way they can when they get something on you. Between growing so fast [Doug is 6′ 10″ today], wearing pants that were too short, and having other kids see me paying at the grocery store with food stamps, I decided to get a job."

Doug was only 13, but he told the manager of a shoe store that he was 16. He sold enough Earth Shoes to become the store's leading salesperson and paid for his family's food and rent. The height that helped him get his first job later helped him earn a college basketball scholarship. He graduated with a degree in marketing and business administration, and took a job as an underwriter with an insurance company.

To earn extra money on weekends, he roofed with his friend Glen Paine. Like Doug, Glen was raised by a single mother on welfare, and had started working when he was 13. He was competitive, driven to succeed, and focused on how to roof faster, longer, harder, and better.

Doug, on the other hand, had no great love for roofing. "There's nothing pretty about it," he says. "It's hard on you and it's dangerous." But everybody needed a roof, the job paid well—and Doug did not envision spending the rest of his life with his full-time employer. "I saw people who had spent 20, 25, 30 years forced into early retirement," he says. "I wasn't going to dedicate my life to climbing the corporate ladder just to have it pulled out from underneath me someday."

Doug quit his underwriting job, and he and Glen decided to start a roofing company. "Glen already had the experience, but I picked roofing for an odd reason," Doug says. "I figured an average guy like me might have a chance at being great at it."

Doug talked his mother into putting up her home as security for a contractor's license. Glen supplied a few tools and a

20-year-old flatbed pickup painted with black primer. In November 1987, Tile Technology Roofing Company opened in Tacoma, Washington.

REDEFINING SUCCESS

Tile Tech was founded on a simple principle: "Do what you're going to do when you say you're going to do it."

"At the time, nobody in the roofing industry seemed to follow through with what they said they were going to do," Doug explains. "If you said, 'I'll be there on Wednesday,' that meant anywhere between Wednesday and the following Monday. It drove me crazy. Glen and I thought, 'If you just do what you say you're gonna do, I don't see how you could lose.'"

For its first five years, Tile Tech's only form of advertising was to do a good job. "We didn't have a number in the phone book, we had zero advertising, no names or phone numbers on our vehicles," Glen says. "We just kept our word and followed through."

In Tile Tech's first year, it made $750,000 in revenues and $100,000 in pretax profit. By 1999, annual revenues exceeded $10 million, Tile Tech employed 100 people, and it was developing a strong regional reputation for its roofs on homes, hotels, hospitals, apartments, and government buildings. Two highly respected professionals, Bob Deaton and Don Vose, also had joined the Tile Tech ownership team.

Poised for growth, Tile Tech sank hundreds of thousands of dollars into equipment needed to win larger roofing contracts.

But when the company, along with its competitors, encountered a shortage of experienced roofers, it realized that long-term relationships with its employees were the key to its success.

Roofing was not a business built on lasting relationships. Most companies gave its new roofers minimal training, made them pay for their own tools, and set them to work with little or no supervision. Not surprisingly, many young roofers lived from paycheck to paycheck and drifted from company to company. Most companies also paid roofers by each piece they completed, which encouraged speed over quality, especially among inexperienced workers.

"There are some terrible recent roof jobs out there," a columnist wrote in the *Seattle Times*. "These are not roofs installed by the Fly-By-Night Roofing Co., the guys who offer that exclusive 'until-your-check-has-cleared-or-you-can't-see-my-taillights' warranty. These are roofs installed by companies with good reputations."

Tile Tech decided to do things differently. It reorganized its roofing teams into a mixture of salaried, hourly, and piece-work employees. The salaried supervisors made sure the team did a quality job and taught the new roofers, who were paid by the hour. Only experienced roofers, who knew how to do the job right *and* fast, were paid by the piece. Tile Tech also created a new career ladder for its roofers that tied their income to training, performance, and leadership skills.

"Rather than being in denial about this endemic problem," the *Seattle Times* columnist later wrote, Tile Tech has "stepped up and done something to change it. Bravo."

CHOOSING A LEGACY

Tile Tech was just as interested in helping its employees develop skills beyond the workplace. Roofing is a hard job and it often attracts people with hard lives. "Some of our guys have grown up in difficult family situations," Doug explains. "Many of them are afraid to show any kind of emotion. You walk up to greet them and I don't know if they've ever been hugged before. Some have had problems with alcohol."

As Tile Tech become successful, Doug, by his own admission, went "a little crazy, I bought some nice toys, house, car—stuff. But I realized that wasn't what happiness really was. I remembered as a kid, being with my family, at school and church—that was where I found happiness.

"As we expanded, I wanted to learn how to treat people properly and encourage them to grow." Doug began investing in himself, reading books and attending seminars, and he discovered a world of wisdom that was open to anyone with the desire to seek it. "It raised my awareness about a lot of things. Glen and I saw that our company wasn't roofs or assets; it was people. We saw that maybe we could help other people raise their awareness. Not trying to change anyone, just letting them know that they had choices in their lives."

Tile Tech became active in community work. When the company heard about an elderly woman whose roof was so rotten that parts of it would blow off in strong winds, it helped replace it and cleaned up her yard. Tile Tech did not forget about its own community either. The company sponsored contests that invited employees to volunteer in their communities, avoid alcohol and chemical dependency, be safe at work, pursue personal goals—"things as simple as bringing flowers to your wife or girlfriend once in a while," Doug says. "If employees want to talk about it, we've gone down about every path there is—addiction, relationships, marriage, children."

With every roof it installs, Tile Tech leaves a legacy. "But the big one is the legacy we're leaving for our children," says Doug.

SPEAKING THEIR LANGUAGE

Soon the walls of Tile Tech were covered with motivational quotes and pictures of employee accomplishments—not the kind of decor that most roofing companies chose. Still, something was missing. "It was like the gears weren't quite in sync," Doug says. "I'd say 20 percent of the employees were really into what we were trying to accomplish, but the other 80 were on the fence."

Then the management team heard a talk about the World Famous Pike Place Fish market. They had all visited the market—Seattle was not far away—and thought it seemed like a great place to work, but they didn't know why. The speaker explained that every day, every moment, each of the fishmongers took personal responsibility for choosing the actions and attitudes they brought to work.

Tile Tech's leaders immediately saw how much the fishmongers had in common with their roofing crews—mostly young men doing a job few others wanted to do. Yet the fish-mongers magically remade their environment through the power of their attitudes.

"It absolutely hit home with us," Bob Deaton explains. "Sometimes we deal with rain, wind, or snow. Sometimes it's too cold or too hot. Are you going to be upset every single day?"

When Bob told his roofers about the fishmongers, they walked out of the office on a cloud. "They could not wait to get back to work," he said. "Suddenly we had words for what we were trying to do."

When Russ Vieselmeyer saw the fishmongers in action, he thought, "They're talkin' right to me."

For employees like Brian Marchel, it was an invitation he had been waiting for. "I've always had a lifelong dream of being a positive person. As a kid, I had kind of a negative step-father," he says. "I stood up to him one day and I told him, 'I'm tired of you focusing on what I don't do, and you never say anything good about what I do.'"

Brian posted the words "Choose Your Attitude" on his front door. "As I walk out, I choose my attitude right then and there," he says. "Sometimes I don't wake up until I get about halfway to work, but then it kicks in."

CREATING AWARENESS

But Tile Tech's employees soon learned that what seems obvious is less easy to put into practice every day. At an early meeting to discuss how to transform their work, a woman announced, "You *can't* choose a @#$&%!! good attitude *every* day!"

Bob Deaton, who was leading the session, had to give her points for honesty. "There's truth in that," he told the rest of the employees. "But you do choose *some* type of attitude every day."

Bob began sharing strategies. "I read that to create a new habit you have to do something for 21 straight days," he told employees. "It's easy to say you're going to do it, but after a couple of days, you're right back to your old habits. To help me remember every day, I started putting a note next to my alarm radio: 'Choose an Attitude.'"

He also told employees to close their eyes. "If you were being promoted and you were going to hire someone to do your job, picture the perfect employee," he said. "What time would they come in? How would they be prepared? How would they talk about people? How would they perform their job?

"Now open your eyes and be that person. Because if you're that, you're awesome."

Throughout Tile Tech, people started to change their days through the power of choice. "Now when I get in the car in the morning, I do a quick assessment of how my day is going to go," says office manager Lisa Franklin. "I ask myself, 'Why I am there? What am I doing it for? What's important to me?'

"Because sometimes you may be having your first cup of coffee, and chatting with someone. If you're not ready and your brain is not on, you might get caught off guard. Your response might not be the best or might not be taken well."

And good attitudes spread quickly. "I started dispatching the guys to their jobs in the mornings," Bob says. "Before, I would have dreaded that assignment. There would be 60 to 70 roofers in here, most of 'em red-faced—and more cuss words than you can imagine. Now everybody comes in, pats each other on the back, says good morning. It's fun to come in. It's like meeting with your friends."

SHARING YOURSELF

Tile Tech's employees also learned that while a good attitude may be great, you need to share it with others. "Before, you'd come to work early, with your game face on, and you'd go right into your office and start working," Bob explains. "You wouldn't even pay attention to other people, maybe say 'Hey' once in a while."

No one at Tile Tech exemplified that culture more than Bob Deaton. "I'd be sitting at my desk, working on a bid, and someone would come up to me with a question or needing something," he recalls. "In the past I would say, 'Not now! I'm in the middle of something!' I basically blew them off without realizing it; I would not even remember they were there."

When Bob saw how the employees of Pike Place Fish work hard to be there for the people they serve, a light came on in his head. "I realized how wrong I was. I had to apologize to a lot of people. I realized it doesn't take much extra time to say good morning to people. I saw how much it means to walk over to new employees, shake their hand, and say, 'Welcome. How are you doing?'"

"Bob has really changed," says Heidi McCaig, human resources director. "He was crabby. But now he makes time for others and he's a good coach."

"This morning I was talking with one of our employees about the fact that he is becoming so focused on his work that he's walking past people without acknowledging them, and being in a hurry with folks," Bob says. "I told him, 'You have the Bob Deaton syndrome. You're being like I was.'

"He sat back, thought for a moment, and said, 'Wow, that really hits home, because I know how I felt about you. I was afraid to come near you. I'm gonna take more time for people.'"

THE SHREWSBERRY GREETING

Mornings at Tile Tech, which has its offices located in a remodeled rambler home with a swimming pool in the back, begins with coffee and the Ray Shrewsberry greeting. "I'm an upbeat guy, and roofers, you know, can be kind of gruff and stern," Ray, a quality control supervisor, explains. "So if I saw someone who wasn't as happy as I thought they should be, I'd yell out their full name, like 'Good morning, Bob Deaton!'"

"Every day this guy would walk past me and say, 'Good morning, Bob Deaton!' It brought a smile to my face every day," Bob says. "So we thought we should all try it. It was amazing how many employees there are whose full names you don't know, so it really helped us to learn them."

The people of Tile Tech are just as serious as they ever were about doing their work; they've just found a way to do it in a lighthearted way. "We have a little stuffed fish, and one of our guys, who has tattoos, pierced the fish's ear and gave him a tattoo," says Tim O'Brien, installation coordinator. "The other day, I had two phones going. One of my coworkers walked into my office, set the fish on my desk, and didn't say anything.

"She answered phones all the time, so she knew how many calls I was getting that day. It just made my day for her to do that. It was a little thing she did that made me feel better and got me through that time."

There's a more lighthearted approach among the roofing crews too. "We don't shoot staples at each other with the fastening guns anymore," says Brian. "Mostly we play through conversation, teasing each other and mentally picking each other up."

Sometimes Doug shows up at the job site with motorized scooters. "It doesn't have a darn thing to do with roofing," he explains. "But you should see these guys' faces when we take a break and have races."

LEARNING NEW TRICKS

Dwight Lambert is in his early 50s. His hair began heading north years ago, and his face is etched with years of hard weather and harder work. You wouldn't figure Dwight to be a

Britney Spears fan, yet there he is, tapping his toes to a Britney tune with a little girl outside her home before he climbs back on her parents' roof.

Dwight used to be known around Tile Tech as "the grouchy old guy," and as he admits, "I guess maybe I had reasons to be grouchy."

Dwight's parents divorced as he was about to become a teenager. His mother remarried, but "I figured my stepfather married her for her and not for me, and that was my attitude," he says. "I just kind of took the bull by the horns and did my own life."

He quit school after his sophomore year and went to work. He was a barber for a time, then worked steel, but whatever he did, he strove to be the best he could be. "My dad told me, 'If all you're gonna do is shovel horse manure, just be the best horse-manure shoveler you can be,' and I've done that all my life."

Dwight began roofing when he was in his mid-30s, an age when many roofers start looking for work that is easier on the body. But he worked smart and he excelled. He didn't even mind bad weather, he says, "because it separates the men from the boys."

It never occurred to him that he could enjoy his work, or enjoy the people he worked with. "For 17 years it was just me and the world. I went out and did my own thing. If you gave me a job, I didn't ask questions. I did it right and I got paid for it."

Sometimes, when working with others who didn't measure up to his exacting standards and exhausting pace, Dwight barked at them. "I guess starting out at an early age, having to think for myself all the time, I was too serious," he says. "Big things I can handle, but little things bother me, waste of time, petty crap. It really bothers me."

One day he was working with his sons and became upset with one of them. "I stomped over to him—we weren't wearing any safety equipment—and I slipped on a loose shingle. I lost my balance and fell feet first." On the way down he hit a $4'' \times 12''$ beam. "I broke my foot and had three screws put in it. I was down for nine months.

"It was one of those things that shouldn't have upset me, and maybe if I had taken an anger management class or something, it wouldn't have, but back then it was like, 'You don't like it? I don't care.'"

Dwight came to work for Tile Tech a few years ago, but he stayed less than a week. "Dwight was extremely dependable and he knew how to do the job," says Doug. "But he turned heads right away with 'This is the way I've always done it and you guys should be doing it my way.'"

Dwight later came back to Tile Tech, but this time he was introduced to how the fishmongers approach their work. "I thought it was silly at first," he says. "But I started to think about how it relates to real life. It brought me an awareness that life can be easier.

"I'm a product of my environment. I've never been in an environment where anyone really gives a damn, other than, 'Are you done? Here's the next one.' They say you can't teach an old dog new tricks. Well, maybe I'm the example that you can. Like I said, it wasn't that I didn't want to; I was just never in that position where anybody could slow me down enough to show me. But I think I was always looking for that. And now I am that."

Make no mistake, Dwight is intensely serious about his work, and he's not afraid to tell you how they *used* to do it. "Old school," the young guys call it. But more and more he's there for his young crew when they need him, sharing the experience he's gathered over the years. He's trying to have more fun at lunchtime. He wears safety equipment. He taps his toes to Britney Spears.

"Sometimes you gotta bark to get some people's attention; then again, if you learn other ways, it isn't necessary," he says. "You can have fun and get as much done and not be all upset at the end of the day.

"Life doesn't have to be that complicated. Twenty years ago, if someone cut in front of me on the highway, I'd holler and give hand motions. Now I just kind of chuckle, 'What's the hurry?' One more car ahead of me isn't gonna make any difference in my day."

Because now there are more important things to think about, like grandchildren. "I've got eight of 'em," Dwight says. "My oldest son's girlfriend has two sons. The oldest one, Andrew, said to me, 'Is it all right if I call you Grandpa Dwight?'

"It brought tears to my eyes. He doesn't have a grandpa. I said to him, 'I'd like it if you called me Grandpa Dwight.'"

Last spring, his wife, Kathy, underwent emergency surgery to repair a bleeding aneurysm. "I just about lost the most important person in my life," he says. "So me coming to work and getting upset . . . hey, no big deal."

STAYING SAFE FOR OTHERS

According to the Department of Labor and Industries, roofing is one of the most dangerous occupations.

When Doug applied for Tile Tech's roofing license in 1987, he says, "the state didn't say boo about safety. I didn't know what safety was, I didn't know you needed it, and then we found out the hard way. The state started enforcing and we got some violations."

Today Tile Tech has a safety committee, elected by its employees, that conducts a comprehensive training program with the Department of Labor and Industries. On angled roofs, employees wear full-body harnesses anchored to the truss.

Yet the decision to practice safety is ultimately an individual choice. "My philosophy has always been: 'If you don't respect yourself to work safely today, call me,'" Doug says. "'There won't be any penalty, you can go home today.'"

Tile Tech borrowed a technique from Pike Place Fish to increase safety awareness. "When one of the fish guys yells out an order, all the other fishmongers repeat it," Russ says. "Before we step on a roof, we walk around the job site. As we call out safety steps and possible hazards, the guys repeat it in cadence. When we do that, we know the guys have heard it. There's awareness."

And they have fun with it. A small swale prompts a cry of

"Thirty-foot ditch! Thirty-foot ditch! Thirty-foot ditch!" If someone is about to toss a piece of broken tile to the ground, he shouts, "Headache!" and the rest of the crew respond in turn, "Headache! Headache!"

Safety coordinator Steve Wallace travels from site to site, checking to make sure Tile Tech crews practice safety, "but I try to catch them doing positive things and praise them for it."

Tile Tech reminds its employees that safety isn't about protecting yourself from something. It's about protecting yourself *for* something. "We have had family nights where we invite spouses to learn more about our philosophies," Doug says. "I explain that I don't ever want to have to knock on their doors and tell them that their husband or son is not going to come home anymore. By using love, we've been able to get through to our people. Now they've caught onto it and it's become their idea."

In 1999, Tile Tech recorded 42 injuries. In 2000, it had 27. Through July 2001, the company had just 5 injuries, putting it on pace to finish with fewer than 10 for the year.

"SOMETHING'S DIFFERENT ABOUT YOU GUYS"

"In the past people would look out their windows and wonder what we were doing," Bob says. "[Our] mentality was: 'Leave us alone! We know what we're doing. You'll see the job when it's done.'"

Today Tile Tech has completely reversed that approach. If customers are interested, its roofing team leaders come down and ask if they have questions. "Instead of looking at it as another roof, we try to remember that it's their dream. We try to make them part of it. We invite them, if they want, to pound a nail in the roof. Heck, when home builders pour the concrete slab, they should invite customers to have their kids put in their initials. People remember things like that. They'll tell friends, 'I helped put on that roof,' and they'll never forget you for that."

When you are focused on another person, and not just yourself, little details take on greater importance. A customer once wrote a glowing testimonial to Tile Tech; his roof looked great, but what really caught his eye was watching one of the crew take the time to remove small pieces of the old roof from the flower garden.

"Before, the guys used to think it didn't matter how [they] acted or what [they] said or did, as long as the job got done," Bob says. "Now they realize how their attitude has a huge impact on the way people perceive our company."

"It's about being considerate," Russ says. "Some companies only clean up the site when the job is done. We clean up every night."

One day, after an exhausting 12-hour day on a roof, one of the guys climbed down and offered to play catch with the customer's son. "They threw the ball around for a while," recalls Brian. "It just totally astonished the customer and made his day."

Making someone's day doesn't end when the roof is on. "I used to call every customer when we were done with the job,"

Doug says. "I'd say, 'This is the owner of Tile Tech and I'd like to know how we did. I want to know the good and the bad.' This blew people away. They would say, 'You gotta be kidding me! Nobody does this anymore!'"

Today Tile Tech goes a step further. "In roofing, it's what you *don't* see that matters," explains Glen. "I bring a digital camera, climb on the roof, and take pictures of the job, then I go over the job with the client.

"I met with an older lady the other day. Her first question was, 'Did you guys leave garbage in my gutters?' I said, 'That's the first picture I took. Look at how clean your gutters are.' She couldn't climb up on her roof to check, and that was a huge thing to her."

There was a time when Tile Tech's customers, like those of most roofing companies, paid reluctantly. "Today that's never an issue," Glen says. "They look forward to paying their bill."

"I don't know what it is about you guys," a customer said after Dwight Lambert's crew had finished her roof. "But something's different. You've brought a new face to the construction industry."

COACHING THE VISION

At a company meeting in May 2000, Tile Tech added two words to its official name; the company is now known as *World Famous* Tile Technology Roofing.

But to become world famous, Doug cautioned, they would have to help each other. They would have to coach each other.

"Coaching is very much a burden," he told everyone. "You can't walk by a problem. When you see something that's not right, when you see broken tiles on a roof, or a truck tire that's low, don't just walk by it.

"And you won't let it go if you take ownership. It's your vision. Don't think that it's just my vision or Glen's or Bob's or Don's. This is for everybody. It's like a relationship. How's it going to work if one person is the boss all the time? It doesn't work, does it? So when we accept the invitation into our vision, we accept two responsibilities. One is to coach and the other is to be coachable."

Asking Tile Tech's employees to coach the owners was not easy. "I think our biggest battles have been giving people confidence that we will respect their coaching," Doug says. "That's not natural in corporate America. People have been programmed to think the owner is not going to listen to them."

Bob calls it "pigeon management. You dump all over people, fly away, wait for 'em to make a mistake, and come back and dump on 'em again.

"When I started in this business 21 years ago, you kept your mouth shut, the boss yelled at you, and you worked. That's just how I was taught. I thought as long as you showed up earlier than anyone else and outworked them, that was a good manager."

But Bob learned it doesn't matter who the words come from; all that matters are the words being spoken. "I was having a loud conversation by the front desk and one of the employees asked if I could go somewhere else because one of the people answering the phones couldn't hear. I started to say, 'Are you trying to tell me what to do?' Then I stopped and asked myself if she was right. Yes, she was."

"I accepted some coaching from our office manager yesterday, and it was so helpful," Don Vose says. "That's a great thing when your employees have the confidence to come to ownership and say, 'I think you're doing something wrong.' And it's even better when ownership says, 'You're right.'"

Glen handled the challenge by being honest with his feelings. "Doug is comfortable in the lead role. I was the guy behind the scenes, but I was definitely in control there."

So when it came time to accept coaching from others, Glen said, "I'm new at this. Don't expect me to be perfect the first time, or the second or the third. I want to be a great listener, a great team player, and to be coachable—but I'm not there yet, so bear with me. So bring the coaching on. I'm gonna grit my teeth and hope I don't say the wrong thing.

"I never used to be a good listener. I didn't look into people's eyes. But I am getting better, especially with my wife and two-year-old daughter. I think the guys see a difference in me too. I used to have kind of a chip on my shoulder, where I didn't let people get too close to me. Now they see me changing, and it changes the way they go out the door."

GOING INTO THE POND

The leadership of Tile Tech once heard the poet David Whyte talk about *Beowulf*, the great epic in which the hero decides he must descend into a lake to battle a swamp-dwelling monster. That lake, Whyte says, is inside each of us. Our fear of going into that lake, into the difficult conversations it represents, can be so overwhelming that we would rather live unhappily than to descend into the lake to find the happiness, honesty, and healed relationships that may await us there.

"When you work closely with people every day, it's easy to become upset with someone or upset others," Bob says. "Those incidents can turn into grudges, and go on and on until you can't even remember the minor incident that happened."

That's why Tile Tech created the Pond. The Pond is a room in the back of the office. Inside is a small plastic swimming pool with sand and an umbrella, a few posters, and two chairs.

"The Pond is for when you need to have a conversation with someone," Bob says. "Maybe someone stepped on your toes, or you think they're not listening to you, or they're doing something that's not consistent with our vision of being world famous. You have the right to ask any person, regardless of their rank in the company, to go to the Pond. There you are on equal ground, and you can say what's on your mind: 'This is what you said or did, and this is how it made me feel.'"

There are no rules in the Pond, except to be respectful. You can be there for 15 minutes or two hours, whatever it takes. "You must be willing to speak your truth, and if you are judgmental or have a hidden agenda, or beat around the bush, the Pond doesn't work," Doug says. "You have to let go of your ego and your sense of righteousness; otherwise you are undermining the power of the Pond."

"Sometimes couples, friends, family members will have disagreements and they give up. They stop talking," Lisa says. "In the Pond we have to finish. In some situations it may be that we agree to disagree but we reach a conclusion."

"When there's a problem, you have to bring closure to it, because until you have closure you cannot go back to creating world famous," Bob says. "It's also important if you're a manager and an employee takes you to the Pond, to not strike back negatively. Because you'll have ruined them and they will never do it again."

Not everyone is comfortable with the Pond, but many have used it. Tile Tech's owners have all been taken to the Pond, and they have taken people there. Damaged relationships have been healed, and new relationships created. Conversations in the Pond have led people to make changes that helped them earn promotions; they also led an employee to leave Tile Tech because he was not comfortable with its direction. Some employees say the lessons of the Pond have helped them to communicate more effectively with their spouses and children.

"It's like going onstage," says Lisa, who was a professional singer before joining Tile Tech. "You pour your heart and soul into your song, to the people who are listening. They might clap and they might boo. You don't know what's going to happen, but you have to put it out there.

"Once you do it, it feels so good. I have yet to be in a position where I've poured out my heart and not gotten a good response. It may not be a fun response, but it's a response that in the end makes me feel better."

"Today we have cell phones and pagers—you name it—but we don't really communicate with the people in our lives," Doug says. "The Pond is a private time, almost a sacred time. It's your time to connect with another person. And we are starting to connect with each other."

TILE TECH'S SECRET

One of Tile Tech's employees had been having some personal problems, so Doug, a close friend, invited him to church. "About halfway through the sermon, he leans over and says, 'Did you tell the preacher what to say today? Because he's speakin' right to me.'

"I just chuckled. We think that we're the only one who's going through this problem, and really we're not. We all share common problems."

And common dreams. "Roofers have feelings and questions and emotions. They want to be part of a great enterprise where they matter and their opinion matters," Glen says. "Once we started using their opinions we became a better company."

That's why Tile Tech puts as much as $250,000 into employee development a year. "Trust me, the return has been tenfold that," Doug says.

"It's not real common in our industry to do that, and while most people really appreciate it, in some cases they don't. That's OK. It has to be unconditional. We take our gambles, but it can be a transient industry, and we invest a lot of time and money into people who turn away. But all it takes is a few people to make it work. They're like seeds; they will grow and touch others.

"Taking responsibility for your attitude and working with others and 'growing' other people, that's a big burden. If you come to our company, you are expected to grow other people once you've grown yourself. We have the opportunity to lift each other up, through all the peaks and valleys, and that's how we're going to get where we want to go together.

"At our Christmas party last year, Glenn Robb, our sales manager, came up to me and said, 'I figured out your secret.' I looked at him kind of funny and he goes, 'You guys figured out how to use love in your business.'

"I just winked at him and left it at that. I didn't have to say anything. I'd known for years what it was."

SMALL BITES

✂ "MOMMY, IT'S RAINING!" ✂

One of our favorite stories is of a six-year-old British girl whose mother introduced her to the FISH! Philosophy. A week later the little girl was getting ready for school on a dreary day. As she was about to leave for the bus stop she said, "Mommy, it's raining outside, but I'm going to have a FISH! day." The principle of choosing your attitude is clearly within the reach of a six-year-old.

✂ WHAT DO YOU OWN? ✂

A parable: Three neighbors were talking when the subject of possessions came up. "I own a huge mansion!" one proudly proclaimed. "I own a successful farm!" said the second. "I have optimism," the third said quietly. His two neighbors laughed at him, for what good is a possession that cannot be seen or touched?

That night a huge storm struck. The storm destroyed the first neighbor's house. "What am I to do?" he cried. The storm ruined the second neighbor's crops. "What will I do?" he lamented. The storm also destroyed the third neighbor's home and farm. "Hmmm, what should I do first?" he asked himself and then he began doing it. He rebuilt his home and replanted his crops.

His neighbors had been sitting this entire time, feeling sorry for themselves. But they watched their neighbor rebuild and they decided to ask him his secret. "It is no secret," the man said. "The only thing I own is what I think." The two neighbors suddenly understood, and with the third neighbor's help, they rebuilt too.

From then on, whenever they met, they did not talk about possessions. They talked about their blessings, and they shared them, for what sense does it make to hold on to something you do not own?

WITH ARMS WIDE OPEN

We recently read about a little boy with a rare digestive disorder. He spent much of his time in the hospital, with needles in his arms. When a doctor or nurse approached him, he knew it was because they were probably going to have to put another needle in his arm. But instead of crying, he smiled and held out his arms for them.

Life can sometimes be painful when you greet it with arms extended. But there is no other way to fully embrace life.

☒ "YOU KNOW THAT GUY BEAR?" ☒

With his gravelly voice, husky build, and face full of hair, Bear is one of the most recognizable fishmongers. Bear understands the power of choice. "You gotta choose where you're gonna be as soon as you get out of the bed," he says. "I do consciously make that choice every day."

One day we got a call from a gravelly-voiced employee at an automobile manufacturing plant. "You know that guy Bear—the guy who looks like he could kick your butt?" he growled amiably. "That's me." But now, every morning before the auto worker came to work, he said, he looked in the mirror and *chose* who he was going to be that day. "I've been coming to work here for 20 years, and if I can do it, so can these young guys."

☒ SAVING A RELATIONSHIP ☒

A woman at a seminar wanted to share her story with us. She told of a marriage on the rocks and growing bitterness between two people who had once felt close. With nothing to lose, she chose to bring the FISH! Philosophy into her fading relationship with her husband. One day she would try to make his day. The next she tried to create lighthearted experiences. When she started listening deeply to him, the effect was powerful; neither one of them had been there for the other for some time. He began to reciprocate.

We followed up with the woman months later. She and

her husband had still decided to follow through with the divorce. We were surprised, for we had somehow expected a fairy-tale ending. But life does not always proceed according to plan. The woman had still chosen to make a difference, and because of her action, all of the anger was gone. Now, instead of two warring adults going to battle, they were two caring adults who had decided to go their separate ways. The lessons of the fish market had not saved a marriage, but they had saved a friendship.

✄ EVEN ON TUESDAYS ✄

After a large school district adopted the lessons of the fish market to help bring more passion to its work, a skeptical school board member happened to be in Seattle during the week. He visited Pike Place Fish, and he discovered all the energy and wholeheartedness he had thought was not possible. "I thought this was a weekend thing," he said. "I didn't expect this to be real on a Tuesday afternoon." Every new day requires a new choice: Who are you going to be today?

✄ A MONKEY ON YOUR BACK ✄

Did you sleep late? Was getting the kids to school a battle? Was traffic horrible? At one hospital, if you show up in a less-than-happy mood, you are invited to wear a stuffed monkey on your back. It's a way of acknowledging the state of mind that's weighing you down—and you cannot change what you are thinking until you become aware of it.

✂ ROCKS, SKIS, AND HOPE ✂

It was 1978, and a young college professor felt his life was falling apart. He was recently divorced, barely had a dime to his name, and his former wife had moved away from Idaho with their sons. All he had were some rocks he and his sons had collected on the day before they left. Somehow they gave him a little hope.

One day the young professor's father bought him some skis, poles, boots, and a lift ticket. The young man fell down the hill all morning. At one point some of his students, who were skiing with him, circled around him. "Get up!" they said. Something welled up inside him; it felt like hope. He got up and skied down the hill for the first time. He skied all day. It was one of the most exhilarating days of his life. On the last run, knowing that the day was ending and he would be working the next day, he said out loud, "I work like I ski!" He wrote those words on a sign and put it in his office.

His sons soon returned to Idaho, and with their father, they enjoyed a life of skiing together. The young professor tried to pay his father back for the skis, but his father refused. "Just pass it on," he said. The professor, who is now a university dean, tries to pass it on every chance he gets.

The rocks are still sitting in a bowl on his desk, and they always will be.

Section Five—LET'S GO FISH!ING

FISH! for 12 weeks and discover the richer and more rewarding life that is just a few choices away.

This section is designed for those who wish to bring the FISH! Philosophy into their lives and would like a few ideas. Included are 12 weeks' worth of activities. Some of these have been field-tested with unsuspecting students and seminar participants, but most are presented here for the first time.

As you work through these exercises, remember that Full Life = Work Life + The Rest of Life. It may seem like a silly reminder. Of course life at work is part of a full life. Yet many of us find ourselves devaluing our work life when we treat it as something we must pass through on the way to the rest of life. For instance:

➤ Are there things at work you take for granted but without these things your life would have less abundance?

➤ Are there times you are doing one thing and already thinking about the next, thereby losing all that the present moment has to offer?

➤ Are there people who serve you every day whom you don't really see and without whom much of what you take for granted would come to a halt?

Now it is time to claim the one work life that is yours to live fully. OK, it may take more than 12 weeks—but the following exercises are a start.

Week One: FISH! Swim Best in a Sea of Gratitude

My daughter Melanie participated in the Semester at Sea program during her junior year at Santa Clara University. The SS *Universe Explorer* sailed from Vancouver with 600+ students from over 240 different universities to spend 100 days at sea visiting 10 countries. Yes, they actually got credit for this.

When she arrived in Kobe, Japan, she wrote to us about sushi and other minor trips outside the comfort zone. As the voyage progressed, however, the nature of the e-mails and phone calls changed dramatically. With visits to Vietnam, China, Malaysia, and India, she and her friends realized they were seeing the USA and their own lives from a new perspective. They would sit up late at night on the deck and talk about the gratitude they felt for the life they had.

As they continued on to Africa, Brazil, and Cuba, the nature of the conversation changed again as these young adults made some interesting observations. They noticed that everywhere they went, encountering a range of standards of living, they found smiling and happy people who cherished family and friends. This was perhaps the biggest revelation of the trip. Life may play out in a setting with or without an abundance of goods and services, but except in circumstances of true hardship, the setting in no way correlates with the quality of the human life it contains. The quality of life is a choice that can be made outside of a discussion of your 401k. A flat tire won't ruin your day if you can feel grateful, not only for the gift of transportation, but also for the gift of life.

HAPPINESS IS A SERIOUS PROBLEM

Author and LA talk-show host Dennis Prager says happiness is a serious problem. He suggests that when we rise in the morning we should notice the many blessings present each day that often go unnoticed. For example, right now your liver is very likely performing well. There is no reason you should take that for granted, but you become accustomed to a variety of important things that are really gifts. The only road to happiness is gratitude for the many blessings present in our lives. You should know that a full and happy life comes more quickly to those who find themselves swimming in a sea of gratitude. If you can create a deep sense of gratitude for the many blessings in your life you will be in the very best position to FISH!

EXERCISE

This week keep a gratitude journal, where you make daily records of the things for which you are grateful. Pay special attention to the important things you may have been taking for granted, but which could disappear in a heartbeat. Do this faithfully and by the end of the week you will be in a FISH! frame of mind. Then continue the process for the rest of your life.

In the box that follows, record some of the most interesting things you became aware of being grateful for, and share them with a friend on the weekend. By the way, don't forget to be grateful for the biggest gift of all: life itself.

Neat Stuff for Which I Am Grateful . . .

Week Two: Conduct a Full FISH! Inventory and Set Some Goals

Below you will find the OfFISH!ial FISH! Scale. Look it over, and while you are doing that, think about the place where you work. Close your eyes and see the people there, watch the activity, and assess the mood on a typical day. After you have taken a good look at your workplace in your mind's eye, think about the stories in this book. Consider play at Sprint and compare your work setting to a playful, fun, light-hearted place. Think about Rochester Ford and the way they emphasize "make their day." Do the same with Missouri Baptist and ponder the way that great caregivers can learn to "be there." How does your workplace compare? Finally, revisit Tile Tech and "choose your attitude." Now complete the inventory below by circling the number that best represents how your work setting compares to the environment at the market and those described in the stories. Look at the anchor statements to guide your choices.

FiSH! TALES

EXERCISE: PART ONE

Play   1   2   3   4   5

1   This place is so uptight that play is a four-letter word.

5   The atmosphere here is lighthearted and playful. It brings a smile to my face just thinking about it.

Make Their Day   1   2   3   4   5

1   Customers and colleagues are treated with indifference or as an interruption.

5   Customers and colleagues are treated in a way that leaves them feeling special.

Be There   1   2   3   4   5

1   People here seem so distracted it is hard to know if they are listening.

5   You are the sole focus of attention when talking with someone here.

Choose Your Attitude   1   2   3   4   5

1   Workers demonstrate the mental maturity of a two-year-old having a bad day.

5   There is a high level of accountability, and everyone knows she or he chooses her or his attitude.

Great! Now you are ready for the hard part.

EXERCISE: PART TWO

Pick the principle whose rating you would like to improve and write a statement about it below. For example, you might write, "I chose the 2 that I gave 'Make Their Day' because I think there is a lot of room for improvement."

Now set some goals and make some commitments about what you will do this week to move that category in a positive direction. These need to be things you can do without anyone else's help. List a couple of goals to start.

Example: I will choose two coworkers and look for an opportunity to do something special for them.

Example: I will find ways to create lightheartedness in my disposition.

Now it is your turn.

1.

2.

3.

Week Three: Find Ways to
Play at Work

This is an easy week. At the market they throw fish, chant, and joke with customers. At Sprint they do the Chicken Dance, take disco breaks, and celebrate each other's accomplishments. As one of the fish guys said, "There are a million ways to play. It doesn't have to be throwing a fish."

This week your job is to make a list of as many ways to play as you can think of, or until you think of 50. Remember, it is about doing things that create a lighthearted feeling at work. Observe the person who lightens the mood when they enter the room. Pretend you are an explorer in an unknown land looking for fun. Start recording your ideas and observations. I will even help you a bit.

EXERCISE:

1.   4.

2.   5.

3.   6.

7.

8.

9.

10.

11.

12.

13.

14.

15.

16.

17.

18.

19.

20.

21.

22.

23.

24.

25.

26.

27.

28.

29. Crazy hat day

30.

31.

32.

33.

34.

35.

36.

37.

38.

39.

40.

41.

42. Post family pictures in the hall.

43.

44.

45.

46.

47.

48.

49.

50.

Week Four: Have Some Fun!

This week is dedicated to having some fun with last week's ideas. Take five of the ideas you listed last week and implement one each day this work week. If your work week is longer than five days, then "Get a life!" Just kidding. If you work Saturdays, then pick six. No big deal.

Remember that play operates in a context of "Make Their Day," "Be There," and "Choose Your Attitude." If you keep that in mind, your play will not be inappropriate. Pulling a chair out from under someone with a bad back might seem playful, but it is not likely to make that person's day.

EXERCISE

In the boxes that follow, record some of the week's highlights.

FiSH! TALES

At the end of the week, tell a colleague about your experiences.

148

Week Five: Intend to Make Someone's Day

The fish guys at the market *intend* to make someone's day every day. They have learned that when you have an intention, opportunities show up. At Tile Tech they discovered a great way to make the crew's day and have a little fun besides. Doug went out to a job site midday and surprised the crew with three motorized scooters to ride. It provided a great break in the day and a powerful message from the boss that employees are valued.

EXERCISE

Think of people in your life whose day you would like to make. List their names below, and when an idea emerges, write it down. Then, when the time is right, go for it.

⚞

FiSH! TALES

I intend to make this person's day. My idea is . . .

1. Name: **Idea:**

2. Name: **Idea:**

3. Name: **Idea:**

4. Name: **Idea:**

5. Name: **Idea:**

6. Name: **Idea:**

7. Name: **Idea:**

Week Six: Random Acts of
Kindness and Cows

After Carr Hagerman and I visited a company in Dodge-ville, Wisconsin, Carr decided to rent a car (yes, his name is really Carr) and drive back to Minneapolis rather than take the plane out of Madison. When I next saw him he told me the following story.

He was on Highway 52, just outside of Rochester, Min-nesota, when he saw brake lights ahead. The cause of the slow-down was soon obvious. Twelve cows were loose on the roadside and appeared ready to cross the road to enjoy the green grass in the center median. They would start across and a truck would sail by, startling them back to the side of the road, where they would build up their courage to try again.

Being a city kid, Carr saw the opportunity of a lifetime and was soon herding cows by waving his hands and yelling, "Yee-haw!" The cows moved away from the highway but remained in a dangerous spot, still blocking a sharply curving feeder road. Carr recognized the danger posed by this blind entrance and doubled his energy. Soon, all the cows were contentedly chewing their cud as they surrounded Carr on a tick-and-horsefly-infested hillside. As the cows crowded Carr, curious about his cell phone, a motorcycle piloted by a helmetless rider rocketed around the curving feeder road just a bit slower than the speed of sound, merged onto Highway 52, and disappeared into the distance.

Carr stood there—frantically scratching—thinking about the enormity of what had just happened. The young man will never know that a total stranger probably saved his life. They will never meet and exchange greetings. As the good feeling of a job well done filled his body, Carr had another thought that was a bit more humbling. "I wonder how long the list would be if it contained the names of everyone who has done something important and anonymous for me."

EXERCISE

> This week is dedicated to random acts of kindness at a place they are greatly needed: at work. At the end of the week you are allowed to write down your favorite random act of kindness and tell a friend about it.

My favorite random act of kindness was . . .

Week Seven: Why Can't We Just Be Where We Are?

One of my favorite writers is a creative spirit named SARK. On my refrigerator is a colorful note card with one of her quotes. It reminds me of something so important and so easy to forget. She writes, "Why can't we just be where we are?"

The fish guys are not selling fish. They are working to improve the quality of life on the planet, one engagement at a time. And they sell a lot of fish. This is not something they could accomplish while distracted, disinterested, while talking on a cell phone or disengaged. They are present physically for their customers—and they are also present in spirit. They know how to "be where they are."

CHRISTMAS IN JULY

I once had a fascinating conversation with my friend Jerry McNellis. As a child he had polio and spent large amounts of time in Gillette Children's Hospital, in St. Paul. It was the day of the iron lung, and the Salk vaccine was just around the corner but of no help for these kids.

I didn't know Jerry when he was at Gillette, but we became friends later in life. I asked him about his time at Gillette and about the visitors who came through. During the holidays Gillette was overrun with well-intentioned people who distributed goodies and quick uncomfortable smiles as they moved through the hospital. The holidays were, for these visitors, a time to do "something" for the kids with crippling disorders. But for the kids, most of the visits were an ordeal, since they lacked one key quality: engagement. Very few of those who visited during the holidays took the time to interact with the kids. It was more like an anonymous parade with candy.

There were, however, two groups that brought the kids great joy, not just at the holidays but during the year. One was a dance troupe whose members danced with the kids. The other was a group of kids with emotional problems from St. Peter Hospital. The kids from St. Peter came in July to celebrate Christmas in July. When they visited, they played, talked, and interacted with the kids from Gillette. They were fully present. That is the power of "being there." It transforms the human dynamic.

EXERCISE

This week is dedicated to being where you are. Think of all the people with whom you interact each week at work. Consider all the work settings you visit. This activity is designed to make all of those interactions more effective, less anxious, and more pleasant.

Below are some ideas that you may either try or use to stimulate your own. After each episode, ask the person for whom you are "being there" if they would mind reflecting on the experience. This reflective feedback will help you catch any little distractions and sharpen your ability to be where you are.

"BE THERE" IDEAS:

🐟 When someone comes into your office to talk, either say, "This is not a good time," or shut down your computer monitor and unplug or ignore your phone while conversing with the person in front of you. If you need to take a call, explain that ahead of time. Move around your desk into a good "be-there" position.

🐟 Always disclose the amount of time you have for a conversation and ask if it is enough.

🐟 When making quick exchanges in the hall, position your body so all you can see is the other person.

🐟 During conversations, clear your mind of everything but the topic at hand, then do it again and then again.

🐟 Never take a cell phone to lunch unless you are at the Motorola Technology Convention. In that case, take it but keep it off.

🐟 If you are in an open area, try not to look past the person with whom you are speaking.

🐟 Use the person's name as often as you can without getting weird.

🐟

🐟

🐟

🐟

A WEEK SEVEN BONUS: *DON'T SWEAT THE SMALL STUFF*

This week, be mindful as an aid to being there. Treat yourself by reading the delightful little book titled *Don't Sweat the Small Stuff . . . and It's All Small Stuff*, by Richard Carlson, in order to understand the power you have over distracting and negative thoughts. Thoughts can't be controlled. They will appear in your mind without warning. Your power lies not in controlling your thoughts, but in choosing not to dwell on them. You can let them go and therefore reduce the impact they have on you as you work to "be there" for another. When you apply this power you will earn an advanced degree in "be there." Take a moment to record the implications for yourself of one or two of Carlson's stories.

Week Eight: How Fascinating! Be There Now!

For over 30 years, Tony Buzan, the creator of a system called mind mapping, has surprised and delighted audiences with two words: How fascinating! In his use of juggling as a metaphor for learning, he will drop the ball and say, "How fascinating!" His message is that dropping the ball is an important event in the learning process. Without it, learning could not occur. Rather than call it a failure or say, "Oh bleep, I dropped the bleeping ball," it is more appropriate to say, "How fascinating!", pick it up, and try again. And in learning, it is important to drop the ball well.

In a high-velocity world, "be there" is a complex skill. The distractions and pressures to take your eye off the task at hand and get pulled into the surrounding chaos are overwhelming. When it happens, you need to say, "How fascinating! I was intending to go to Charleston, West Virginia—not Charleston, South Carolina! How fascinating! I will try again."

When my first daughter, Beth, was about four years old she asked me if we could go to the park. I said sure. It was

something I wanted to do, but with the heavy travel schedule I
had at the time, I put it off until the next weekend. A year later
I realized I had yet to take her to the park. I told this story as a
part of my presentation to the American Heart Association
and a week later received an e-mail from a young father of two
boys. He said that for a year he had been telling his boys that he
would camp out in the backyard with them. My story created
an awareness in him, and he said to himself, "How fascinating!
I love my boys and love doing things with them and it has been
a year since we first discussed camping out in the backyard."
They camped out that night.

Being there requires an awareness that penetrates the
stress and chaos that is a part of our world. You will mess up,
and when you do, the only reasonable thing to say is, "How
fascinating!" Now try again.

EXERCISE: IN THIS MOMENT

The first assignment this week is to read this quote from
Thomas Merton:

*The rush and the pressure of modern life are a form, per-
haps the most common form, of innate violence. To allow
oneself to be carried away by a multitude of conflicting
concerns, to surrender to too many demands, to commit
oneself to too many projects, to want to help everyone in
everything is to succumb to violence. More than that it is
cooperation with violence. The frenzy of the activist neu-
tralizes his work for peace. It destroys her inner capacity
for peace. It destroys the fruitfulness of his own work*

because it kills the root of inner wisdom which makes work fruitful.

EXERCISE

Spend the rest of the week working to be one place at a time and to learn the most powerful lesson in the universe. There is little tension or anxiety in the place we call the present. And if you find yourself worrying about things in the future, say, "How fascinating!" Then take a deep breath and return to the now. And if you find yourself working on one project but thinking of another say, "How fascinating!" Then take a deep breath and choose the project that will be the sole focus of your attention. And if you find that your anxiety about everything you have to do is keeping you from going to the park with your daughter, sitting and talking to your spouse, or camping in the backyard, take a deep breath, say, "How fascinating!" and return to the now. It is a marvelous place to be. You may decide to work or you may decide to go to the park; either is just fine as long as you are wholeheartedly present. Just don't sit and be anxious. That has no value at all. How fascinating!

WEEK EIGHT BONUS: *THE POWER OF NOW*

If you find yourself wanting a little more on this important subject, let me suggest *The Power of Now*, by Eckhart Tolle. He shares such wisdom in this book that I keep it close to my desk at all times. I find that I can open it to any page and be rewarded with an insight.

Clearly, Tolle understands the damage that is caused by spending too much time in the future and the past. With great clarity he describes the peace and tranquility that can only be found when you are in the now. Open this book anywhere and enjoy. If you are like me it will stay on your desk for a long time.

EXERCISE

> After you have made a few excursions into the writing of Tolle, capture some of your insights here:

Week Nine:
Do You Have a Full Deck?

I have learned a great deal from my colleague Carr Hagerman, but perhaps the most powerful lesson comes from his experience in the theatre. One day he said, "Someone who is acting is not interesting. An actor needs to *be* the person whose role he or she is playing."

I have thought a lot about this lesson from the theatre. Great actors don't "act"; they assume the emotions, feelings, and personality of the character. This to me is evidence of the power we each have to choose. Romeo and Juliet may have driven through terrible traffic and had arguments with their significant others, but you see none of that when they are onstage. We each have that capability!

In preparation for your greatest role—your own life—you might copy this idea from the theatre. Consider developing a deck of cards from which to choose your attitude. These cards would contain the name of an attitude on one side and, on the other side, words, pictures, or phrases that are helpful in producing the internal state of that attitude. In other words, "being the attitude."

If my attitude of choice is serenity, I might have a picture of my favorite listening point on Lake Superior. If patient, I can picture the quivering stillness of my dog Bo as I hold a treat in my hand. He will hold that position for hours if he needs to. If I want to create more selfless and unconditional love in my life, then a picture of Mother Teresa is perfect. If I want the attitude of wholeheartedness, then the waxing and the waning of the moon in the poem *Faith* by David Whyte will remind me that I need to have equal faith in my joys and in my grief.

EXERCISE

There are two exercises this week, and you probably have anticipated the first. Prepare the first five cards in your attitude deck. Three-by-five note cards are perfect for this task. Out of all the possible choices, pick five attitudes you would like to see more often in your life.

After you have prepared the cards, simply look at them at set intervals during the day, perhaps hourly or perhaps when the phone rings. Each time, ask yourself this question: "What attitude do I have right now—and would I be better off with one of the five in my hand?" If you don't like the one you have, choose another, but first write down the name of the one you have as best you can.

Record of Attitude Checks

The Attitude I Have:	The Attitude I Choose:
✖	
✖	
✖	
✖	
✖	
✖	
✖	
✖	
✖	
✖	
✖	
✖	
✖	
✖	
✖	
✖	
✖	
✖	
✖	

Week Ten: It's Not about Choosing a Positive Attitude

An engineering firm in Southern California and a clothing manufacturer in the Midwest have an interesting connection. They each have produced a wall of attitude buttons from which to choose. Attached to the wall are some of the most marvelous attitudes: Peaceful, Patient, Positive, Energetic, Caring, Sensitive, Productive, and Loving. The one that is always checked out, however, is "Pissed Off."

The idea to consider this week is that it is not about choosing a *positive* attitude. It is about choosing. There will be times when the weight of life is so great that you make a less-than-spectacular choice. It is called being human. But if you can stay connected to the fact that whatever attitude you have, it is the one you are choosing right now, then the awareness itself will move you in a more satisfying direction.

Take a lesson from the Duchess and Diva of Distribution at ChartHouse. (At ChartHouse we create our own titles. It is one of the lighthearted things we do.) Wendy and Gwen manage the network of distributors for the company, a demanding task. They have a map of the world on the wall and a white board on the office door where they post their attitude each morning. I love to go by and see the daily choice. Occasionally I will see "Frustrated" or "Melancholy" written on the board, but more often it is "Confident" or "Energetic." Whatever it is, the fact that it is posted reminds the Duchess and Diva—as well as all those who walk by—that they choose their attitude. Remember, whatever your attitude at the moment, it is the one you are presently choosing.

EXERCISE

This week's exercise is simple but powerful. Put a white board up on your office door or near your desk, and regularly post your attitude for all to see. See if your example leads others to start posting theirs below yours.

Week Eleven: Who Are You Being While You Are Doing Whatever You Are Doing? Why Not Set a World Record?

This is as good a time as any to tell you that I am a world record holder. Really! Today you might see me as bald, out of shape, 235 pounds, and in my 60s. There was a time when I was bald, out of shape, 235 pounds, and in my 50s.

In 1993, I went to Lafayette, Louisiana, to compete in the Hubba Bubba Road Race. It was the five-mile world championship for "Clydesdales." In order to qualify as a Clydesdale in the men's division, you had to weigh in excess of 200 pounds, and my 235 easily qualified me. As I lined up at the starting line I was inspired by the fact there were only five of us in my over-50 division—I could tell who the others were by the color coding on their numbers. I had already taken the measure of two competitors and felt confident they carried in excess of 250 pounds, giving them a definite disadvantage. That is, if they didn't step on my foot at the start.

The gun fired and the ground shook as the mass of meat shot from the starting line. At mile one, three of my competitors were struggling as we passed the marker in 7 minutes and 15 seconds—a blistering pace. I tucked in behind the man in fourth and dug deep into my reserves in order to hold the pace. As we approached the finish line and I prepared to go into my famous kick, my competitor stumbled over a young 300-pounder who had abruptly stopped right in the middle of the road. I raced by on his blind side and finished a full second in front of him, in a hot time of 35:40, to become world champion.

That was the last time the Hubba Bubba world championship five miler was held and so, to this day, I remain the reigning world champion. The point? If you find a small enough pond you can be a big FISH! Did you know you are not only world champion, but hold the world record for being you? And to make it even better, every time you improve on you, a new record is established. Why not shoot high?

WE ALL DO STUFF, BUT WHO ARE WE BEING WHILE WE DO STUFF?

This eleventh week is dedicated to improving the many world records you already hold. How about setting a new team-member record? Perhaps this is the week you improve your record for positive contribution to the department. This is a week to set some new world records for you.

Top decorative fish symbol

✂ FISH! TALES

EXERCISE

If you need a boost to get started, ask yourself, "Who would I be if I was being world-record me?" Do that for all of your major roles and keep a record of the highlights for use during your next performance review. Why not?

The Role I Am Playing . . .	My New World Record . . .

Week Twelve: Tag, You're It!
Light Some FISH! Fires

The first year I was a counselor at Camp Courage I was assigned to the young boys' cabin, Cabin 3. The eight- and nine-year-olds filling our cabin to the brim with energy brought with them a devastating variety of disabling conditions but a common upbeat spirit. I will never forget Beaver.

Beaver was a bucktoothed eight-year-old with muscular dystrophy. He slouched in his wheelchair because he lacked the muscle strength to sit up. On the second day of camp the ever-smiling Beaver announced he wanted to go on a hike—not on the tar paths that crisscrossed camp but through the woods. When you are a 17-year-old counselor you figure ways to do things you wouldn't consider later in life. We wrapped Beaver in beach towels to keep him safe and set off cross-country with the entire cabin in tow. Imagine a single-file line through the brush with four wheelchairs and a half dozen sets of crutches. An hour later we returned with an excited group of young boys, and Beaver could speak of nothing else. I heard that he talked about that hike all the way home at the end of camp.

The next summer I looked for Beaver's file as I prepared for the first group of campers. But Beaver had not made it through the winter. He simply grew too weak to keep going.

I think a lot about the campers who didn't come back the next summer, football teammates who didn't return from Vietnam, and other friends who have gone before me. Life is so precious, and yet we often seem as if we are passing through work on the way to another place, never really in the life we have at the moment. What a waste!

The last assignment is to live each moment fully. To live in a way that honors the preciousness of life itself. To live in a way that attracts the attention of others as they see and feel your passion for life. Perhaps your example will inspire a real conversation, and one more person will see the possibilities that follow an understanding that "life is too precious to just be passing through."

EXERCISE

Find something to wear that reminds you of your commitment to living your life fully and that causes others to comment and ask you, "What is that about?" Each time someone asks you why you are wearing an octopus on your head, or whatever, you have an opportunity to recommit to your personal vision and at the same time start a small fire in the heart and spirit of another. Over time you will find your commitment deepening.

When others ask why you are so upbeat, tell them about the choice you are making! It may help them see their own choices.

And when you are blessed with an opportunity to help

another human being to see her or his potential, take a minute to do that. It may be the most powerful legacy you leave on this earth.

It is my hope for you that you catch your limit of life—every day!

FISH! STICKS™

INTRODUCTION

Some say change is difficult. I say change is a piece of cake (or perhaps cheese). If you want a real challenge, try to *sustain* a change—especially a change that requires commitment from all who do the work.

It doesn't matter if you are an individual contributor who wants to hang on to a better work life or a CEO who wants to maintain a new high level of productivity: Sustaining change is the true test of leadership. Holding on to a culture of innovation, maintaining a higher quality of work life, constantly renewing an important customer service program, or retaining a more participative management style requires the use of a unique set of principles that are different from those used simply to initiate a change.

A large-scale change usually comes with a lot of fanfare, so in the beginning there is considerable energy. It's typical to have meetings, training programs, off-sites, balloons, buttons, contests, pocket cards, newsletter articles, posters, and videos. And there is absolutely nothing wrong with any of these. External energy is often what it takes to catch our attention in a busy world. But external energy cannot sustain a change. That takes a different source of energy: natural energy.

When the balloons have deflated, the contests have ended, the training is complete, and the natural human tendency to look for the next new thing has started to exert itself, that is when the inevitable gravity pull of old ways sets in. When you are part of such an effort it feels like someone just took her foot off of the accelerator.

This gravity pull takes many forms, including distraction, busyness, resistance, boredom, forgetfulness, cynicism, and sabotage, to name a few. It doesn't really matter what is at stake—a new diet or a new way to be at work—all worthwhile changes are susceptible to the forces of gravity. Successful efforts to counteract these forces in order to sustain change is what separates the great workplaces and great people from the pack.

After teaching change management to MBA and corporate seminar students for twenty years and operating my own business in an environment where change was a constant, I coauthored the book *FISH!* and worked on a film of the same name. Ever since, I have had the privilege of observing organizations using the ideas in *FISH!* (as well as principles from other management books) to address a variety of important issues and to create positive change. The most pressing workplace needs addressed by those who turn to the FISH! Philosophy include improving the quality of work life, customer service, employee retention, the facility for innovation, productivity, and recruitment. Another reason people turn to it is simply to learn how to have more fun at work.

Over the last three years I have traveled almost a million miles speaking to and visiting with those who, in one way or another, are working to implement important organizational changes. I have been especially inspired by change efforts that were sustained after the excitement of the initial rollout had waned. There is a bounty of energy present when something is new—but a year later it takes a deeper source of energy to keep it going. I have seen many successful organizations that have found that source. Any wisdom demonstrated by the characters in this book has been extracted from real people sustaining change in real organizations. The World Famous Pike

Place Fish market, the inspiration for *FISH!*, is of course one of the many ongoing success stories from which we have learned valuable lessons.

This book is the work of my imagination, but it is based on many experiences the three of us have had over the last few years. John Christensen continues to make FISH! the main focus of his company, ChartHouse International, a place where stories are routinely collected in the course of business and where the language of possibilities rules. Harry Paul has found a life on the road speaking and consulting about FISH! It is a rare day that Harry doesn't have something to share.

Yes, we now stand on the shoulders of thousands who have brought new possibilities into their workplaces and their lives. Some have failed, some have succeeded, and for many it is too early to tell. But we have learned from them all. *FISH! STICKS* is designed to highlight the special set of commitments involved in keeping *any* worthwhile change alive. It is truly your story: I just happened to write it.

Stephen C. Lundin
Lutsen, Minnesota, USA
Fall 2002

External energy is necessary at the beginning of any large-scale change initiative. To implement a new vision, you must first have everyone's attention.

But external energy is only effective for the short term. Eventually, external energy must be replaced by natural energy in order for the change to stick.

Brunch at Brunch

Rhonda and Will Bullock have a Sunday routine. Rhonda sings in a gospel choir and Will sits in the first pew with the kids. Then it's off to the nursing home to spend some time with Grandma. On special Sundays, like today, the next stop is the mall, where the kids chow down on fast food while Rhonda and Will look on in amazement during the ninety seconds it takes the kids to make the food disappear. Then Will walks the kids and the baby-sitter to the cinema while Rhonda waits in line for a booth at a wonderful little restaurant called, appropriately, *Brunch*.

This Sunday as Rhonda waited in line for Will to return, her mind drifted to the Good Samaritan Hospital, cornerstone of the Good Samaritan Hospital System of two dozen hospitals and clinics throughout New Jersey and the whole tristate region. Good Samaritan had been her employer for eleven years, and as she thought about work she could feel herself growing tense.

"Hey. Do I detect a frown instead of the usual smile?"

"You caught me thinking about Good Samaritan, Will. Sorry. I'm guilty of violating our number one rule for Sunday: no work. . . . Did you have any trouble finding a movie suitable for an eleven-year-old boy who thinks he is an adult and a seven-year-old girl who brings her doll to the theater?"

"The usual. Mike tried to convince me that *Return of Shaft* would be a good movie to see even though it is R rated. He said Shaft could be a great role model, and he promised he would hold his hands over his sister's eyes during the bad parts. Mia was willing to go wherever her big brother suggested, of course, but I explained that they needed to find a G or PG movie. They settled on the new Harry Potter film. Ann said it was great."

For a brief moment Rhonda saw the shining face of her wonderful stepdaughter, Ann, now twenty-eight and living in Los Angeles.

As Rhonda and Will settled into their booth and ordered, Will studied his wife closely. He knew something
was really bothering her. His nickname for her was "Happy
Face," because she was one of the most upbeat people he
knew. She could have a cranky service-person showing her
pictures of family members minutes after their first words.
Today was unusual, for her mood was clearly dark.

"Forget our Sunday rule, Rhonda. Do you want to talk
about what's wrong at work?"

"Will, I'm failing in my new job."

"I'm sure that can't be true," Will replied immediately.

"It is. It really is. When Madeleine left and I was promoted, I tried not to let myself worry about whether I
could live up to her remarkable example. Madeleine was
my idol; I worshiped that woman. She brought life to a dismal hospital ward, a place where nobody wanted to work
because of the dreary atmosphere and lethargic people,
and she helped it become the crown jewel of Good Samaritan. We still have bigshots coming from all over the hospital and even from other hospitals to study our success.
Madeleine helped us see that the sixth-floor neuro ward
didn't need to be an unpleasant and uninviting place; that
we could make it a better place to work and a much better
place to be a patient. And with her leadership we did.

"I remember so clearly the old days, before Madeleine

became head nurse on the ward. I dreaded going to work even though I have always loved nursing. I had tried to maintain my usual positive attitude but it was hard. Every night when I came home, I was mentally and physically exhausted. You remember.

"Then, one day, Madeleine was promoted and immediately caught our attention by showing us a film and passing out a book for us to read. The title was so odd, we thought she was joking. She used the principles in that film and book to help us see how we could create a better place to live at work."

As Rhonda paused for a bite of her meal, Will asked, "Isn't a key word in that story 'we'? Didn't Madeleine really rely on *you* to help her? Weren't you two all alone in your beliefs for a while?" Will remembered Rhonda's frustration with her coworkers, who were deeply suspicious of any attempt to influence them. "Just another program," they said. "This too will pass." And the famous, "Been there, Done that, and Got the T-shirt."

Rhonda finished chewing and picked up the conversation. "That's true, but I can't blame the others for being wary. Health care has had so many changes that people have become cynical and resistant to being jerked around again. Once everyone realized that this wasn't just another program but more of an invitation to team up and create something really cool, then the energy started to build pretty quickly. It wasn't long before people in other parts of the hospital took notice. Madeleine became kind of a celebrity. We joked that she started a positive 'staff infection' of joy, caring, and compassion. That's when she began to help other parts of the hospital system, and that's why they asked her to become a consultant to hospitals all up and down the East Coast."

"Rhonda, I know all that. I know she's a dynamo; but so are you. She gives you a lot of credit, you know. And she told everyone she has total confidence in your ability to take over from her running the neuro ward."

"I know, I know. And I believe I did make a real contribution. But now that I have her job, I'm beginning to wonder if I can keep the energy going. This week I started to doubt that I can."

"Something happen?"

"There's an aide I hired just three weeks ago, named Juan. Well, yesterday Juan told me he liked what we were doing in neuro, but just didn't feel a part of it, and so he asked me to help him get a transfer. Will, he is just the kind of competent, caring aide we need on our ward, and he doesn't want to stay! I must be doing something terribly wrong. We have had attrition before, but it has been two years since we lost someone to another unit. We still have a waiting list of people who want to come to work on six. But this seems like a warning that we are reverting to old ways. And there are other things that worry me."

"Such as?"

"Some things are hard to describe, but you can feel the difference in energy level on the ward. I don't hear quite the spirit in the nurses' voices. And the call lights seem to be staying on longer and longer before anyone responds. You don't see nurses offering to help other nurses as often, and when there is a nasty task to do the staff seems to evaporate.

"Last week a patient with a morphine drip vomited, and I just happened to be the first person to walk past his room. After I pressed the call button for him, it was ages before anyone came to help me get him cleaned and in a new gown."

"I get the picture, darling. But you have to admit you have really high standards. Perhaps this is just a momentary thing. You have some new staff and a couple nurses out on maternity leave, so it might take a bit to get the new people up to speed."

"I hope you're right, Will. What is hard for me is that

I have been entrusted with something that was working and now it is not working quite as well. It feels like a personal failure."

A Good Samaritan Monday Morning

The sixth floor was swirling with activity as Rhonda opened the stairwell door and headed for the break room, which contained a coffee machine and a refrigerator used mostly to keep brown-bag meals fresh. As she entered the break room, she acknowledged each of the three people there with a warm "Good morning." Two responded cheerfully. Juan, who was sitting by himself, barely glanced up. *What's going on with Juan?* she thought.

Rhonda then walked from the break room toward her office. On the way there, she passed a number of patient rooms. Two had blinking lights over the door so she stepped into the first to find that Mrs. Swanson simply needed a glass of water. The light over the second door was still blinking when she extricated herself from a very chatty Mrs. Swanson, but as soon as she approached she could see that there were two nurses standing in the room. The beds were occupied by a quiet and rather shy woman named Lois Anderson and her roommate, who must have come in during the night and who was sleeping fitfully.

The two nurses seemed to be discussing a game show and showed no awareness of Lois or the call light. As Rhonda entered the room with a quiet but pleasant "Good morning," the two nurses looked at her with startled expressions.

"Good morning, Rhonda. Did you see the new *Survivor* episode on TV last night? You wouldn't believe the gross stuff they had to eat."

"I am sure I wouldn't," Rhonda replied. "But are either of you aware that Lois's call light is blinking?"

In unison they looked over at Lois, who mumbled, "I need help going to the bathroom."

As one of the two nurses stammered a sheepish, "I'll help you," the other started backing out of the room. Rhonda followed.

"What was that all about, Rob?"

"Sorry, Rhonda. We both watch every episode of *Survivor* and we just got caught up in a discussion about it. It was really extreme."

"In a patient's room, Rob?"

"Not too bright, huh?"

"I'm bothered by your use of a patient room for any

conversation that doesn't involve the patient. And particularly by a conversation about, as you put it, 'gross stuff.' Lois was waiting for help, and you didn't even know that—even though you were in her room. This just isn't the kind of environment we've said we want to create."

Just then, Paul, one of the hardest working orderlies, came up behind them pushing a gurney with a middle-aged man on it. Two bottles were suspended on hooks above the gurney.

"Good morning, Paul. Is this a new patient or a transfer?"

"Mr. Abbot was released from the ICU this morning after a week there. I'm taking him to room 614. There was that accident on the George Washington Bridge last night and the victims were brought to us. I think Mr. Abbot would have spent another day in the ICU otherwise, but they needed the beds."

"I hear you, Paul. We'll need to stay extra alert with Mr. Abbot."

Rhonda spoke into the ear of a mostly unresponsive Mr. Abbot. "We are going to take good care of you here, Mr. Abbot. I'll be down later to see how you are settling in."

Rob had slipped away as she was talking with Paul.

When Rhonda stepped into her office, she was met by the sound of a ringing phone. For the rest of the day the action was nonstop. There were bed shortages, nurses out sick, supply mistakes, families to greet, staff who just needed to talk, grand rounds, training to be scheduled, and on and on. It was well into the afternoon before Rhonda had a chance to think more about her problem and another incident that brought it to mind.

Rhonda was approaching the nurses' station in the center of the sixth floor, where the three wings converge and the elevators are located. She overheard a conversation that reminded her of the old days. Marge, a hard-edged nurse with twenty-five years' experience, was in the process of briefing Beth, a young nurse who had quickly become a leader on the floor. Beth was just beginning her shift.

Rhonda could hear Marge saying, "This guy in 614 is a real pain in the butt. Why didn't they keep him in ICU for another day? His call light is on all the time, and when you go down there you can't understand what he is saying and then he gets all frustrated. This job is hard enough without that crap. Look out for him." Marge then stormed off.

"Hello Beth—was Marge talking about our new patient, Mr. Abbot?"

"Rhonda. I didn't see you come up. I was just getting briefed by Marge on a problem."

"Does the problem happen to be a patient with a name, Beth?"

Beth's mouth dropped open and her face took on a crimson glow. Then she smiled and said, "Busted."

"You're a leader here, Beth, and I don't want to make too much of such a rare slip, but I have a larger concern. Help me understand what's happening if you can. You were the first one to embellish your identification badge to demonstrate your commitment to our new approach to nursing on the sixth floor. And you were there when we saw how our work-lives and the quality of patient care might improve if we brought a lighthearted energy to our work. You were in the front of the pack when we made the choice to be present for our patients and for each other. Now, all over the hospital, you can see other departments following our lead. You were one of a small core that made the early commitment on this floor. But here on six, the place it all began, we seem to be losing it. Is it just me, or is something happening?"

"I really hadn't noticed, Rhonda. You know how excited I am about what we have here. I really look forward to coming to work in the morning. That in and of itself makes it worth the effort. I don't always enjoy the work I am doing—bedpans and IV drips are not enchanting objects. But I always enjoy the way we work together and the way we provide care.

"That story about the fishmongers being fully present for customers really hit home with me, and I saw the implications for my work with patients. But you know, when things get stressful I sometimes forget about the possibilities and simply put my head down and plow ahead. And things are really stressful right now. All the rooms are full and many of the patients require a lot of care. Some of us are totally worn out from the sheer volume of work. Perhaps we have lost our focus, but please understand: I'm not any less positive about what we have created."

"Do you remember what you said about our new way of nursing on six? Do you remember how you framed it?"

"I'm not sure what you are referring to, Rhonda."

"You said as nurses here we always took great care of the *physical* needs of our patients, but that it was time we recognized that our patients bring their *soul and spirit* along with their body. I don't know if I ever told you how much that comment touched me. We have to find a way to hang on to the progress we've made. Our patients bring their soul and spirit with them, Beth, and so do we! If we fall back now, *we* lose out as well."

"We can't fall back, Rhonda. I was drawn to nursing to be that kind of a nurse. But it's hard to remember all this stuff that makes so much sense now, as we stand here talking calmly, when you have a day—a string of days—like I've had. You know that it has been one crisis after another, with too many things to do and not enough help. I'm exhausted and I'm really stressed out. I do want the best for our patients and for us. It's just hard right now."

"I know it's hard," said Rhonda. "I'm starting to wonder if the creation of this high-energy, fun-loving work environment was the easy part. Keeping it going is turning out to be a difficult task."

"Well at least we have something worthwhile to keep going. And we do have an investment to protect. It took a while to create, as you well know."

"You know, Beth, when you think about it, everything needs a little maintenance to keep its value. When my daughter Ann forgot to check the oil in her car she found out the hard way about the relationship between maintenance and value."

"I know what you mean. I have some family silver and I really love the connection with my past. If family members hadn't polished it regularly over the generations it would not have lasted to enhance my life. We polish it for our children and our children's children to enjoy. It takes some work to keep things you value in good shape. That holds true for silver, cars, relationships, and our work life on the sixth floor. I do want to help, Rhonda. But it's not easy. There's just so much work that needs to be done and a limited amount of time and energy."

"I know. But I'm sure we can figure this out."

Just then, Mr. Abbot's light went on. With a vibrant smile, Beth turned and strode down the hall toward his room.

A Timely Phone Call

"May I speak with Margo Carter, please? This is Rhonda Bullock."

"Rhonda, I'm so glad you called. It's been too long. How's life in New Jersey? I talked to Will yesterday. Did he tell you? How are things at work? No, don't answer that. Let's have lunch and catch up. No, let's have dinner. I discovered this neat sushi restaurant in my neighborhood and I want you to experience it. When can we meet? How about this week? What do you think?"

The minute a new way of working is initiated, the gravity pull of old ways begins.

In the beginning, novelty can be an adequate source of energy. Over time a deeper and more sustainable source must be found.

Rhonda was not known as someone at a loss for words, but her oldest friend was a talker. They had known each other since first grade at P.S. 163. After college, Rhonda had moved to New Jersey and Margo had stayed in Manhattan. "That's a great idea, Margo. I'm pretty open. When and where?"

"How about six o'clock Thursday at Takara Too on Sullivan Street. That's in the village between Bleecker and Houston. You'll know you're in the right place if you see a huge line of people waiting to get in. Dress for the weather, because we'll probably stand outside on line for a while. Got to go. See you Thursday."

Rhonda felt like she had run a four-minute mile. *Stand outside for a while; then why go there? Well, it should be interesting. Actually any time with Margo is interesting.*

Takara Too

Come Thursday, Rhonda left the kids with Will and took the Path train into Manhattan. As she walked along Bleecker Street toward Sullivan, she enjoyed the architectural and human diversity in that part of Manhattan, where Soho and Greenwich Village meet.

I forgot how alive the city is in the evening.

When she got to Sullivan, she noticed, on the other side of the street, a nondescript restaurant with an awning over the front door and transparent plastic sheets hanging to the ground. It was barely distinguishable in the darkness that arrives too early on a winter evening. But she could see more than a dozen people standing on line outside the awning and the shadowy forms of a few more behind the plastic drapes.

It was 6:05 as she paused to look at the number she had written down, 824 Sullivan. *That must be the line Margo predicted—but what's the deal with the tacky plastic sheets?*

A yellow cab raced by as she started across the street. On reaching the opposite curb she could make out some faded handwritten letters on the window. *Takara Too*, it whispered.

"Rhonda! Back here!"

At the very end of the line, peeking around a backpack worn by a young man who was hugging his girlfriend in the chilly air, was the face she had seen regularly since she was six years old. She gave Margo a wave.

"What were you doing across the street?" asked Margo.

"Just another suburban woman trying to find her way around the city in which she was born. I really enjoyed the walk from the PATH station. I forgot how interesting this part of the city can be."

"Are you surprised by Takara Too?"

"When you said that people stand on line, I pictured something . . . well something more trendy, I guess."

Just then the line moved and Rhonda took the opportunity to look around while they shuffled a few steps toward the awning. She could see there were space heaters under the hanging plastic sheets. Inside the restaurant she made out a number of long tables stretching from the front to the back, with little room for movement.

"So does my choice of restaurant surprise you?"

"I'm a bit curious. I expected something modern. I guess that's my view of New York hot spots."

"I could show you a number of modern sushi places with ultra hip decor a few blocks from where we stand. And you know what: You wouldn't have to wait on line at any of them. But here the line forms every afternoon at four and it doesn't end until they lock the doors at midnight. Amazing, isn't it?"

They were pleasantly interrupted by a waiter with a tray of sushi to sample. He offered them something he called a New York roll. They savored it for a minute and then Margo continued.

"So how's your new assignment? What's it like having helped create a wonderful new patient-care culture and then finding yourself in charge?"

"I don't want to spoil our dinner by talking about my work problems."

"Problems?"

"Really, Margo, I am so happy to see you and I want to catch up on all you're doing. I'm afraid that once I begin talking about my work problems I won't stop."

"Rhonda, the glue of our long friendship is the fact that we are always there for each other and can always talk about anything. What's going on at work?"

"I'm watching our wonderful new culture, as you call it, slip away from us a little at a time. And I don't know what to do. It's all coming unglued. We seem to be losing our focus as the reality of working in an active hospital reasserts itself.

"There has always been some attrition, Margo. People move, get promoted, go to school, and have families as they always have. But now there is the threat of turnover and we haven't had that for a long time."

"Great distinction! Every time we see each other you talk more like a leader. You're right. Attrition is a fact of life—people move, preferences change, promotions come—but you can have an impact on turnover."

Attrition is a fact of life.

But turnover is preventable.

"Juan, one of the new recruits, doesn't want to stay, and he is exactly the kind of aide we want and need. He told me he loves the energy on the sixth floor but doesn't feel a part of it. It's not that the staff is unfriendly. He says they have all been polite and respectful. It's just that they seem distant. This never would have happened when Madeleine was there. I appreciate your kind words about my leadership, but I'm having some doubts about being able to fill her shoes. There are other signs that the special place we've created for our patients and for ourselves is slipping away. Health care can be a sea of stress, and for a while we created an island of sanity that served as an antidote to that stress. I don't know what to do."

"Rhonda, are you aware that the problems you are facing are quite predictable? You know that if Madeleine were still in charge, she too would be facing them?"

"What do you mean?"

"Well, I have learned in my work that it is one thing to implement change and quite another to make it stick. The gravity pull of old ways starts the minute you initiate something new. When the energy is high, you aren't even aware of the pull. After you have been operational for a while, people lose some of their focus and it takes a different set of commitments and a different type of focus to keep things going. A lot of the early energy comes from things you do, external things like events. Eventually the new way of being will live or die according to the degree an internal source of energy and direction can be established."

"How do you know so much about it?"

"I have some experience with a customer-service project that provided me with a similar challenge. I'll tell you more about it over dinner, but right now I have an admission to make."

"What's that?"

"Remember I said I'd talked to Will the other day? We're here at this restaurant because of that conversation. When I called for you and you weren't in, Will wanted to talk. He told me about your struggle at the hospital. He's quite concerned, you know."

"You talked to Will about me?" Rhonda found herself a bit annoyed at first, but then realized there was nothing to be annoyed about.

"Yes, and if you hadn't happened to call me I would have called you."

"Well, do you really think this challenge would be present regardless of who was in charge? Is it like a cycle or stage you go through? I can't help thinking I'm just not up to this job."

"What you are experiencing is a very, very common problem. The good news is that there are some great examples of people and places that seem to have solved the problem. The line we are now in started forming every day four years ago. That's a very long run by New York standards. When we get inside you will meet Mrs. Ishihara, or Ishy, as she likes to be called, and her husband—if they can find a moment to say hello. They do know we're coming tonight. She has been a delightful mentor to me in my work and I have a hunch she may be helpful to you."

"You have a sushi chef as a mentor in banking."

"Absolutely! She's a great leader, as you'll soon discover. And best of all, she knows how to keep a good thing going."

"If she's a friend of yours then why are we standing in line?"

"It's part of the way she runs her business. Everyone is special here. No one gets a reservation and no one cuts the line."

"So we're here to see how she runs her business?"

"Yes. That's the reason. Ishy ran the family business in Seattle, a restaurant called Takara, but she longed to be a sushi chef. A female sushi chef is as rare as a solar eclipse, but she was determined. Her husband is a sushi chef and a real mensch. While she ran the business, he taught her the trade during their free time. When she felt she was ready, they turned Seattle Takara over to her sister and moved to New York to start Takara Too. Now she has a reputation as one of the best sushi chefs in the U.S."

"Why did she come here?"

"Why not? New York is the eating capital of the world."

The line had moved slowly and they were now in front of the awning. As they pushed aside one of the transparent plastic curtains they were greeted with a rush of warm air. Stepping inside the tent formed by the awning and the hanging plastic sheets, they gave their names to a tall waiter and then took their position behind some of New York's most diverse. In addition to the loving couple there were business suits, grunge wear, enough pierced skin to set off all the metal detectors at LaGuardia, and a Japanese family of four. The tall waiter disappeared like a puff of wind. Then he returned, handed them each a menu, and pointed out the specials, which were printed in small, delicate calligraphy. Margo handed the menu back to Rhonda, saying, "I left my reading glasses at work, so you'll have to read it for me."

The tall waiter smiled and took Margo's menu back from Rhonda. As he softly moved away, everyone stepped back to allow a number of smiling customers to exit the restaurant. And then the tall waiter was back again, holding a beautiful silver tray with six pairs of loaner reading glasses arrayed and marked according to power, weakest to strongest. Margo seemed genuinely surprised, but quickly took a pair of the strongest glasses and thanked the waiter warmly as he once more handed her a menu. She looked at Rhonda, who was watching all this intently, and said, "Always something new here."

Soon, a soft voice said, "Your table is ready."

As they moved into the restaurant, they were met with an enthusiastic Japanese hello and a burst of applause from the entire staff. It was both an exciting and welcoming greeting, and it created a sense of anticipation, perhaps even adventure.

They scrunched into two seats at the end of a row of tables closest to the counter where the sushi was being prepared and quickly smiled at their neighbors—not characteristic New York behavior, but the atmosphere was so intimate it seemed natural. In fact, it generated a couple of return smiles. Behind the counter on a slightly raised platform were four sushi chefs working with quick, controlled movements. They shouted to each other as they prepared the sushi, pausing only to applaud new customers. White stucco, hanging blowfish, hand-lettered signs, a silk-screen tapestry, exposed heating pipes, clean but well-used tables, and not an empty chair in the room—that was the decor. And it was easy to spot Ishy since she was the only woman behind the counter, and she smiled and winked at Margo as they sat.

"Well, what do you think of Takara Too?"

Before Rhonda could answer, a waiter appeared. When they gave him their attention, he asked if they had a drink preference or any questions. They ordered tea and looked at the menu. Then Margo looked up at him and said, "Why don't we turn it over to Ishy?" He smiled his approval. Standing nearby, Ishy chuckled.

Rhonda confided to Margo: "I know sushi is very popular, but I generally prefer soul food and Diet Dr Pepper."

"Trust me—it won't be too unusual and there will be plenty of choices."

"That's fine. Don't worry about me."

The waiter returned with the same calm presence Rhonda had noticed in the demeanor of the tall man at the door and deftly placed the tea on their table. Then he set a Diet Dr Pepper in front of Rhonda, who looked up startled and received a bright smile and a nod.

"I know you don't have that much experience with sushi," said Margo. "But this visit is not about the food, although anything that is served here is of the very highest quality."

"So we're here to meet Ishy?"

"Yes, but that's based on some assumptions I made after talking with Will. If I was wrong, we'll simply have a great meal and catch up. If my assumption was correct, we'll do all of that and meet a remarkable woman who has discovered for herself the keys to sustaining a successful work culture.

"Ishy really saved me when I ran into a problem at the bank, the same kind of problem you now have. I had taken the lead in establishing a new customer-service initiative and it worked so well that we were starting to receive recognition not only within the bank but also from the whole banking profession. I know I bent your ear more than once about that three years ago."

"Oh, that program. Didn't you call it WOW or something like that?"

"Yep. Good memory."

"So what happened to WOW?"

"Well, it all began to unravel at the very same time the bank recognized our work by nominating me for a city-wide leadership training program. You can imagine how stressful and embarrassing that was. I was being honored for something that was, at the same time, falling apart."

"I was a floor nurse then, and remember thinking that management is definitely not for me after I saw what you were going through. Now all I can think is that I should have remained a floor nurse."

"You'll do just fine, Rhonda. If ever there was a natural leader it's you. Anyway, it was in the city-wide leadership program that I met Ishy. Ishy has a way of doing business that keeps people coming back and makes them eager to tell others about their great experience here. Ishy, her husband, and the rest of the crew here have a formula for sustaining their vision for a great sushi restaurant and they are doing it in the most competitive market in the world."

"What's the recipe?"

"Not so fast, Rhonda! Let's just experience Takara Too and then let Ishy set the context. Although I have read many books on the subject, what I know about getting a vision to stick in a real organization with real competitors comes from her."

With that, the first course arrived.

"Ms. Bullock and Ms. Carter, your broiled yellowtail collar," the waiter said as he set a massive piece of fish on the table. "It's good to see you again, Ms. Carter, and I hope you enjoy your first visit to Takara Too, Ms. Bullock. I'll leave you alone between courses unless you remove the small piece of sushi from this pedestal. You can eat it or just remove it and I'll know you need something." He placed a delicate piece of sushi on the miniature pedestal that graced their table.

"Thank you. May I ask you a question"—Rhonda glanced at his name tag—"Tako?"

"Certainly."

"How did you know I wanted a Diet Dr Pepper?"

"I heard you mention it. I can take it back if you don't want it."

"I was dying for a Diet Dr Pepper! Thank you. But I didn't see it listed on your menu under beverages."

"That's because we don't stock it. But there's a deli a block from here that does carry it and I needed the exercise. I hope you enjoy it." The waiter smiled and then went to help a busboy clean an area of a table that had just been vacated.

"Now," said Margo, "let's get down to the business of"

eating. This is the neck of the yellowtail tuna. It's a real delicacy. Grab those chopsticks and give it a try."

"Wait a minute. How did he know my name?"

Margo grinned and responded, "Remember when we were in line the host came over and greeted us?"

"Yes, he took down our names. He also repeated them to see if he pronounced them correctly. I thought that a bit unusual, but I now see the name was passed along to our waiter. When do they do that?"

"I don't know, but it happens seamlessly every time."

They were soon immersed in a sea of wonderful tastes and textures that didn't end until the last piece of sushi was presented and eaten. At one point during the meal their waiter pulled up a camp stool and sat down with them. He didn't ask them if everything was OK, but instead engaged them in a conversation about the sushi. It felt unhurried even though it only lasted a minute.

Vision Moments

"Do you like the sushi?" Rhonda and Margo looked up from their conversation to see Ishy standing by the table.

"It was wonderful, Ishy; I want you to meet my friend

Rhonda. I told you a little bit about her work at Good Samaritan when I called you."

"Welcome to Takara Too, Rhonda. I only have a few moments right now, but I wanted to say hello and tell you I'm available to offer whatever help I can. Margo and I had some fun a couple years ago dreaming up ways to help her bank. I'm sure that preparing sushi and operating a restaurant is much less complicated than health care, but Margo seems to think some of the things we do to stay fresh might be helpful. Do you have any questions?"

"How do you keep people standing in line for four years?"

Ishy broke into a massive smile and said, "One 'vision moment' at a time."

"Vision moment?"

"We have an experience we are working to create here and each of us takes responsibility for that creation. The line of customers could disappear tomorrow for any number of reasons—we all know that. So we live as many vision moments as we can. Margo and I were in a program where they talked a lot about knowing clearly what you are trying to create and finding the vision to communicate your goals. So we call the moments that arise each day that allow us to live the vision for Takara Too, 'vision moments.'"

"I'm sure I just experienced quite a few, but the one I remember is the Diet Dr. Pepper."

"Yes, I saw that. Tako is always looking for ways to do a little extra for our customers."

"It must help to have great sushi, too."

"Absolutely! The quality of the sushi we serve is vitally important, but there are many restaurants that have great sushi. It is the quality of the experience we create for our customers that keeps the line outside from going away. And we are always looking for ways to enhance the experience."

"What is this experience you are creating?"

"You tell me. You experienced it."

"OK. I'll try, but please excuse me if I miss something important. I would say the quality of everything on the menu is a part of it. Margo tells me that if you can't find a high-quality piece of tuna, you don't serve tuna that night. Your understated and eclectic setting is a part of it. The gentle and engaging manner of your waitstaff must be a conscious thing and part of it. And there is also the sample we were graciously offered as we froze our butts off standing on line."

A vision is made manifest in real time by identifying and bringing to life possibilities that are always present. These become "vision moments" once we take action.

Ishy smiled and said, "We ran out of butt warmers just before you arrived. Go on."

"The awning shows a concern for customers and flaunts your popularity in a subtle way. The experience you create with the high-energy greetings and applause is part of it. But what impressed me the most was the unrushed way your waitstaff interacted with us. I felt as if I could stay all night, but you turn tables with regularity. I now realize that your staff let us savor each course, but cleared immediately once we were done. They moved quickly so we didn't have to. How am I doing?"

"You can start tomorrow!" At this they had a good laugh.

Ishy looked directly at Rhonda and continued, "I meant what I said about helping, Rhonda. Let me know. You identified most of the observable features of our vision for a restaurant. The trick, however, as you might expect, is keeping this vision alive by living our individual and collective vision moments. According to Margo, you've made some remarkable changes at Good Samaritan. That's just the beginning. Now it's time for you to put in place the engine of renewal. I'd like to help you if I can."

"So do you suggest that I go back to the hospital and tell people about vision moments?"

"What I suggest is that you and Margo go for a walk and come back in an hour. We'll talk more after I've finished serving my customers. Do you have time to do that?"

Rhonda looked at Margo, who nodded. "Absolutely," said Rhonda. "See you in an hour."

A Sushi Walk

As they stood up, Ishy shouted something in Japanese. The three chefs at the counter repeated it with three grins as Ishy rejoined them. "I wonder what she said, Margo. The chefs clearly got a kick out of it."

"I think she said, 'The wicked witch of sushi returning to work.' They do crazy little things like that once in a while; it keeps life interesting."

After Rhonda called Will to say she'd be home a lot later than planned, she and Margo carefully wove their way to the exit. Rhonda suddenly felt a surge of hope. *Four years*, she thought. *Just maybe . . .*

"Let's go look at the other sushi restaurants in the neighborhood," suggested Margo. And off they went on a tour of three sushi restaurants, all within a few blocks. None of them were very busy even though it was still the peak dinner hour on the busiest weekday. One place that must have cost millions to decorate sat mostly empty.

Margo commented as they looked through the window, "They have the finest décor money can buy, but they haven't been able to create an experience that customers value. I'm sure their sushi is of the highest quality, but they don't have a clear vision. They have a world-class facility, but they haven't been able to create an environment to match.

"Rhonda, you and your staff do have a vision of what you want on the sixth floor. You have created a special experience for patients and staff, a place where the whole person can heal. The next challenge is finding a way to keep alive and vital that experience you have worked so hard to create and to keep yourselves from backsliding."

Real Conversations

Ishy was waiting for them at an empty table off to the side. A few diners were enthusiastically finishing their meals. Rhonda decided to get right to the point given the hour and the fact that they had all gone through a full day.

"If you were in my position, Ishy, where would you begin?"

"I would start with conversations about work and about IT."

"IT? What do you mean by IT?"

"Your IT is your personal piece of the vision. Organizational visions are often written in flowery and abstract language. They need to be written that way because of the many stakeholders involved. But your own IT needs to be more focused, specific, and personal. And you find IT through conversation. In fact that is the only way to find IT.

"So if your vision is a particular philosophy for health care, you find your IT by talking to others about work and about your place within that vision. By the way, I suggest you wait a while before you talk about IT around the hospital. It might actually distract people, because it does sound a bit strange at first, and you can do a lot without mentioning IT."

"You don't need to worry about me. I'm not about to go back and talk about IT before I understand it better. But let me see if I'm getting this: These conversations are about each person's own individual relationship to the special sixth-floor experience we are jointly working to create?"

"Exactly! You might start with questions like: What are *we* creating here with our precious life energy? To what are *we* committed? Then: What is *my* role inside the vision? What is at stake for *me*? You know: questions like that. Deep questions about work that will get people to pause and think about what they do and the way they do it. One of the great things about these deep conversations is that just the act of having the conversations often increases the energy level. Natural energy is released when we talk about things that are important to us. The way we live our life at work is a vital topic, and the energy that sustains change will flow from those conversations. It's a vital topic because we all are aware of the huge amount of time we spend at work."

"I think I experienced something like this earlier this week," said Rhonda. "I started off reprimanding a terrific employee who made a mistake. We wound up having a real conversation. And just that conversation seemed to help her regain her energy.

"May I come back and talk with you again? This feels like an important place to start, but it also feels like the tip of the iceberg."

A quick hug at the station and a promise to talk again soon, and Rhonda was on her way home. On the train she took out a small pad and wrote down a few things. *So much to remember,* she thought.

The only way to find our IT inside the vision is to talk about work with coworkers.

These conversations must be both real and fierce.

Real because they require an authenticity that belies pretense or posturing.

Fierce because the amount of time we spend at work makes these conversations vital to a satisfying life.

Friday flew by and the weekend was one continuous shuttle service for the kids and a long conversation with her stepdaughter, Ann, in LA. The bond between Rhonda and Ann had always been strong and grew stronger each year. Rhonda always felt some sadness after talking with Ann because she so missed having her with them in New Jersey. But she felt less sadness after this call because they were making plans for Ann to come home for a visit.

Contemplating the Week Ahead

The children were in their rooms studying and Rhonda was thinking about work again. She took out her notes from the ride home from Takara Too and reviewed them.

Notes from Dinner with Margo at Takara Too

 Margo says that even if Madeleine were still head nurse on six there would be a need to replace the dependency on external energy with a more natural energy. You can only rely on external energy in the beginning.

🐟 The gravity pull of old habits begins the minute a change is made.

🐟 Ishy has sustained the popular Takara Too experience for four years.

🐟 Ishy is willing to help me with my challenges at Good Samaritan by teaching me more about how they sustain their vision.

🐟 It starts with real conversations.

🐟 The idea of vision moments is intriguing.

🐟 The Diet Dr. Pepper incident was Tako living a vision moment. The reading glasses were also a vision moment.

🐟 We talked about finding our IT inside the vision, but I am not sure I would feel comfortable talking to others about IT.

🐟 The one thing I can do immediately is to start real conversations with the staff at work. I can begin with questions like:

    1) What are we working to create on six?
    2) To what are we committed?
    3) What is our personal role inside the vision?
    4) What does success look like?

5) How will we support each other in keeping from
    backsliding?

➤ So I need to start the conversations. It is a place
to begin in what will surely be a long journey to hold
on to the changes we have made at the hospital.

She put the notes aside for the night, remembering a commitment that she and Ann had made to each other. They vowed they would take some time, no matter how short, for themselves each week. Rhonda realized it was now or not at all.

Ann had given her the complete works of poet David Whyte for her birthday, and she decided to read some of her favorite poems before herding Mike and Mia to the bathroom.

I am fascinated by this man's work. Imagine: a poet who takes his poetry into organizations.

Tonight one poem caught her attention and she read and reread it.

The Journey

BY DAVID WHYTE

Above the mountains
the Geese turn into
the light again

painting their
black silhouettes
on an open sky.

Sometimes everything
has to be
enscribed across
the heavens

so you can find
the one line
already written
inside you.

Sometimes it takes
a great sky
to find that

small, bright
and indescribable

wedge of freedom
in your own heart.

Sometimes with
the bones of the black
sticks left when the fire
has gone out

someone has written
something new
in the ashes
of your life.

You are not leaving
you are arriving.

I am arriving. I am arriving at a new place, a place where none have traveled before in quite the same way and where a unique challenge awaits. I have everything I need but no guarantee of success. We have a good thing going at Good Samaritan and it must be maintained and renewed. Failure is assured if no action is taken. So I will start the real conversations or, as David Whyte would surely suggest, the fierce conversations about the one life that is uniquely ours to live at work.

The First Conversations

"Good morning, Ping."

"Hi, Rhonda. What are you doing in the break room? I hardly ever see you in here taking a break."

"I guess I'm doing what I should have done when I was first promoted. I'm trying to talk with the people who do the work. Ping, I'm interested in your view of what we're trying to create on this ward. Do you mind if we talk for a minute while you drink your coffee?"

"Are you having a problem with my work, Rhonda?" Ping sounded defensive and a bit annoyed.

"Oh, no, Ping. I'm not trying to sneak up on a criticism. Your work continues to be a model for us all. I'm trying to start a conversation that is a bit awkward and unusual. What I want to do is to talk about the work we do and what it means to us. You know: have a real conversation about our work life."

Ping relaxed visibly. "That would be cool, Rhonda. Just give me a second while I get another cup of coffee. Can I get something for you?"

"I'm fine, thanks."

"You want to know my view of what we are creating on the floor. Tell me again exactly what you want to find out?"

"I'm curious about what you are thinking about as you do your work during the day. You're a great nurse, Ping, and you're also fun to work with. What guides you?"

"Thanks. I've always tried to be a *good* nurse, but when Madeleine first got us talking about our choices, I realized I had the opportunity to be a *great* nurse in the same amount of time. And I really do try to maintain a lighthearted demeanor. There are enough people in the hospital who wear their underwear really tight, if you know what I mean?"

"Yes, I've noticed," said Rhonda with a chuckle.

"I also try to really listen to our patients when I'm with them. I try to be 100 percent present during those moments. And I look for little things to do that will make the day brighter for my teammates. I believe I write a key part of my life story at work and I want to write the best story I can."

"Have you noticed that we seem to be losing some of the energy we developed while Madeleine was here?" Rhonda ventured.

"Now that you mention it, Rhonda, yes, I have. It's probably normal, isn't it? I mean nothing lasts forever, does it?"

"Is that what you want?"

"Oh, no! I find working this way so much more satisfying. Before we turned things around I wanted a transfer to the ICU. I also had my resume out to other hospitals. A couple weeks ago Mercy Hospital called me about an opening in their ICU and even offered a signing bonus. I said no because I really don't want to leave. I have an investment here and I love working with this team. Well, most of the team. I definitely don't want to go back to the old boring, bickering, unconscious way we used to work. No way. You remember what it used to be like."

"I sure do, Ping."

"I'll never forget the moment I realized things had to change. I was working with a patient shortly after Madeleine showed us that film about the Seattle fish market. I was changing a dressing, the task I had gone into the room to perform, but continued talking to Heather, who was still in the hall. I happened to look up at the patient and I saw my distraction painted on his face. I decided then and there to be fully present for patients; that the quality of their experience with us is always at stake. But that was only the beginning."

"Go on, Ping."

"I don't know how to say this exactly, but something

happened as I became more and more successful at pushing aside distraction and being fully present in what I was doing. I found my life more satisfying. I was a lot less anxious. What started out as a specific insight about patient care turned into insight about the quality of my whole work experience. I know we have a lot at stake here, Rhonda."

"That's all music to my ears, Ping. Do you mind if I share your story with others here?"

"Sure, Rhonda, but please don't mention my name. That's not what it's about."

"What did you mean, though, when you said you liked working with 'most of the team'?"

"Some of the new people don't seem to get it."

"Do you mean like Juan?"

"You said it. Juan just doesn't fit in."

"Have you ever talked to Juan about what we are trying to create on this ward and why?"

"No. Isn't that a job for management?"

"I'm management now, and if there is something I should have been doing then I've dropped the ball. If we lose Juan, as I fear we might, I think we will have lost someone who could be a great asset. I was in the group that interviewed him; his last employer raved about his energy and enthusiasm. I will do what I can to correct the problem, but I'd really appreciate it if you could take some time to give Juan your perspective and maybe ask him some questions about what he wants in life. If you don't mind, I think it would be great if you could seek out not just Juan but also a couple of our other teammates and have a conversation kind of like the one we are having. I have a couple questions I'm going to use to guide me as I continue to do the same thing."

"Sure. I'm happy to do that. And I would love to know your questions."

"Okay, here they are: What attracted you to health care? What is the Good Samaritan experience we are working to create for patients and staff on the sixth floor? What is our individual contribution to that experience? What is at stake for you?"

During the week, Rhonda hung out in the break room as much as she could. She came early to see the night staff and left late so she could spend some time with the second shift. None of the old-timers wanted to go back to the way things were; they liked the energy on the floor. But the new hires with whom Rhonda spoke said they still felt like outsiders. And no attempt had been made to integrate the three temporary replacements. The temps had been well briefed on their assignments, but no one had bothered to say anything to them about the shared vision for work on the floor.

On Thursday she found Juan alone in the cafeteria and stood next to him with her tray. "Hello, Juan. May I sit with you or would you rather be alone during lunch?"

Juan seemed startled by the question and her presence, but made a welcoming gesture with his arm. "Please join me. I just got here."

Rhonda sat down and they ate silently for a minute or two. Rhonda then broke the silence with, "Have I told you how much you impressed the selection committee?"

"No. That's nice to hear. When I moved to New York after my wife's promotion I had offers from a number of hospitals. This place had my kind of energy. I was surprised it didn't seem to be working out for me."

"Didn't seem to be working out?"

"Well, I felt like an outsider after I got here. You had the toys and posters and stuffed fish everywhere and I wasn't a part of all that. The staff seemed to be having a good time, but it didn't include me. All the neat stuff happened before I arrived. I had a talk with Ping yesterday and I am still in a state of shock. Good shock."

"Oh?"

"She and I had a real 'man-to-man' conversation. You

know what I mean. And I told her I didn't feel a part of things and she told me I came off as aloof. Wow! That stung. But I can sort of see it from her perspective."

"So what are you thinking?"

"Well, I've decided to talk to some other people so I can better understand what makes this place tick. It feels good to be taking more responsibility for how I fit here. I guess it's a two-way thing."

"Let me know if I can be of help."

"Sure, Rhonda. And thanks for telling me that stuff about the selection committee. I needed that."

An announcement interrupted their conversation. "Rhonda Bullock, please report to the sixth floor."

"Got to go, Juan. Duty calls." Rhonda saw a line at the elevator and took the stairs to six where she found a number of nurses using their lunchtime to sing to patients. They wanted her voice and she gladly gave it.

Surprise!

A few weeks had passed since her dinner with Margo at Takara Too, and Rhonda continued to have and encourage conversations about work with the staff. No one was really sure why, but the conversations were having an impact and

some of the old energy was returning. But life was about
to intrude.

"Good morning, Rhonda. This place is colorful."

Rhonda turned to find Phil, the hospital director,
standing with a tall woman wearing a starched white uniform complete with an old-fashioned white nursing hat.
"Good morning, Phil."

"I would like you to meet our new vice president of
nursing, Mable Scallpell. Headquarters has assigned her
to us. As you know, the position has been open for quite
a while, and I'm happy to have it filled by someone so
qualified."

"I'm please to meet you. How would you like to be
addressed?"

"Call me Miss Scallpell, if you don't mind."

"Well, I'll leave you two to get acquainted," said Phil
as he quickly backed away.

"Thanks, Phil," said Rhonda to his back as he moved
hurriedly away. "So where were you before, Miss Scallpell?"

"For the last fifteen years I've been VP for research. It
feels so good to get back to patient care one more time
before I retire. This hospital has such a great reputation
at Headquarters."

"Well, that's good to hear."

"But isn't all this commotion a little disturbing to patients?"

Rhonda felt herself tighten up a bit. "Commotion?"

"The colors, the little plastic fish on the name badges, the toys, the stuff on the wall. I'm sure it distracts people from caring for the patients."

"Actually, our patients seem to appreciate our efforts. And the fish stuff reminds us of the story of the fish market where the employees play; choose their attitude; are truly *present* at work; and make each customer's day."

"I think you should ditch the toys and signs."

"But . . ."

"It's decided. It may be the first decision I've made on this job, but I think it's an important one. I want you to tell your nurses that we are going to do things differently. Get back to a more professional way of nursing. The silly name badges must go. The toys must go. They're just not professional. You might even think about wearing a real nursing uniform like mine. Any questions?"

"Well, I . . ."

"You are new on your job. Not quite a year, right?"

"Yes but . . ."

"You will see it's for the better. I want a report each

week, and you can bring it to my office on Monday morning. We'll talk about your progress then."

You've Got to Be Kidding

"I'd like to see Phil, please."

"He's on the phone. Would you like to make an appointment, Rhonda?"

"I'll wait, thank you."

"I'm not sure when he will be available. Can I . . ."

"Hello, Rhonda," said a very sheepish-looking Phil as he came out of his office. "Come in for a minute."

Rhonda seated herself and got right to the point. "Phil, you knew, didn't you? I could see it on your face. Miss Scallpell is everything we have committed not to be. She has so much starch in her white uniform that if she fell asleep while standing she wouldn't fall over. If you take two 'l's out of her name, it cuts like a knife. You have to be joking. Not now, of all times, just when we are getting back on track. I . . ."

"OK, Rhonda, slow down and let me try to explain. My support for your efforts and the patient-care revolution we have experienced continues. Unfortunately, I do not run the Good Samaritan Hospital System, just this hospital, and this is a system-wide move. Miss Scallpell has the qualifications for the job. She really does want to get back into patient care at the end of her career. There may be some rough edges because she has been away from the hospital setting for a while. But she was a great nurse and is a great administrator."

"Rough edges! She wants me to stop doing anything fun. Too much color, she says. Unprofessional, she says."

"I know it will be a challenge, Rhonda, but hear me out. Miss Scallpell is not unreasonable. I know she wants what is best for the patients."

"One of the reasons I'm so upset about this is that since taking over from Madeleine I've observed a gradual loss of energy and a return to old ways of doing things. We've been working on the problem and we are just starting to make some progress. Now this! She wants us to remove all of the posters, all the toys, all of the visual reminders of what we are about."

Phil shrugged. "Do the best you can, Rhonda. But I'm telling you that Miss Scallpell will be our vice president of nursing for the next eighteen months and will have my full support as long as she has patient care and the well-being of staff as her highest priority. I would like you to make this work. Is that clear?"

"Clear as a bell, Phil. Is the execution at dawn?"

"Cute, Rhonda. I do have one piece of advice. I mean, after all, I am the hospital director and as such I have taken credit for most of the great things done by the nursing staff here."

"Cute, Phil. What is your advice?"

"Try to understand where she is coming from and to see the world through her eyes. And when you are dealing with someone who spent a large portion of her life doing research, use facts, figures, and findings to make your points. I'm already late for a meeting, but I wanted to take this time because I know you have been caught by surprise and I feel some responsibility for that. But I also want you to think about one more thing. If the whole new changed atmosphere really depends entirely on some toys, badges, and posters, then did we really make a significant lasting change for ourselves and our patients? Or did we just redecorate?"

Word Travels Fast

Almost immediately the new regime of Mable Scallpell was the topic of discussion everywhere. In fact, on the elevator ride, one of Rhonda's favorite doctors expressed his support for Rhonda and then, as he rushed out of the elevator door on five and headed down the hall, shouted over his shoulder, "Fight for what you have created, Rhonda. The sixth floor is a great place to work and the perfect environment for patients to heal in."

The first thing Rhonda heard as she arrived on the sixth floor was a nurse saying, "We will revolt. She can't do this to us. We have worked too hard!" And that was still exactly the way Rhonda felt. Recognizing the need for some time to herself, she went to her office and shut the door.

As she sat at her desk, her eyes were drawn to her notes from Takara Too.

. . . you can only rely on external energy in the beginning. . . . you need to replace the external energy with a more natural internal energy. . . .

What's external and what's internal? The posters may be on the wall, but they also remind us of what we are about. Do we actually still see them, or are they now a part of the background? Have we become too accustomed to the fish?

Miss Scallpell may have a point. It might be time to move away from our dependence on "crazy hat day" and all the theme stuff. But how will I ever convince the staff that this isn't one giant step back?

Rhonda decided to hold some small group meetings and to take a positive approach. At the first meeting, she briefly explained the desires of their new boss and then quickly reiterated her hopes for the conversations she had initiated. "I am very encouraged by the conversations we have started having about work," she said.

"What about Miss Scallpell?" chimed in Chelsie with the question that was on everyone's mind. "What does she think about our conversations?"

"She will also benefit from the work we do."

"No, I mean, won't she try to stop us? Talk about stiff!"

"I think we should avoid jumping to conclusions and also avoid discussing someone who isn't present. I caught myself doing that the other day and it's something we said we wouldn't do on six. It creates a negative environment. I plan to take any issues I have with Miss Scallpell directly to her and not to a third party. We need to extend to her the same courtesies we have committed to extending to each other." There were a number of nods.

"What we are doing is good for patients and good for us. We know that because we were here during the transformation to a more human and lighthearted way of nursing on six and we have seen what we started spread to other parts of the hospital. And one thing Miss Scallpell shares with us is a dedication to good patient care."

During the second of these meetings the first question was again about Miss Scallpell. Then Ping signaled she had something to say.

What is Ping doing? Rhonda thought. *I need her support here.* "Yes, Ping."

"Rhonda, I've been thinking about the challenge issued by Miss Scallpell and the investment we've made in this workplace. The conversations you started have gotten me to thinking about what a tragedy it would be if once we created a great place to work, we then let it slip away."

Here we go again. Is Ping going to ask me to fight for the colorful posters and fish?

"We have all contributed to the improvements in our work life and patient care, and therefore we have a lot at stake. But I can't help but wonder if Miss Scallpell's reaction might not be an opportunity in disguise."

"An opportunity, Ping?" There was a disbelieving buzz among the others, but Rhonda was thinking, *Go, girl!*

"Yes. I think we may have become too dependent on the external stuff, anyway. We have a fun committee. We have plastic fish attached to our name tags. We have Hawaiian shirt day. We have theme meals. And we even serve fish candy and fish crackers at our meetings—although the crackers are usually stale. I am not suggesting we give up everything that is fun, but the stuff we do doesn't have the punch it had in the beginning.

"I think we can continue doing some of the wonderful and sometimes outlandish things we do that brighten our days and delight our patients, but perhaps it is time for something more."

Beth jumped in, adding, "I've been thinking the same thing. As long as we rely on external things to keep us juiced, we are at risk. As we have just seen, the externals can be removed on the whim of a new boss. Life has a way of intruding without first asking permission. If we move the source of energy inside and take more personal responsibility for regenerating our lighthearted and service-oriented workplace, then we are more immune to some of the crazy things that can and will happen without warning. The purpose of all the stuff we did was to create a special experience for patients and staff on six. It worked, but it was a means to an end and not an end in itself."

And I was worried about how to stop a riot. Sometimes I underestimate this group.

Rhonda was delighted. Two members of her staff had just summarized the primary lessons she should have just learned from Margo and Ishy. They may already have had that wisdom inside them or it may have been transmitted unconsciously during the conversations; it didn't matter. It was there.

Juan spoke up, "Why don't we put our little plastic fish inside our clothing so it's out of sight? This can be a symbol both of our dedication to keeping our way of working alive and also recognition of our personal responsibility. The fish has gone inside."

There was a short discussion about whether this was external or internal. Ping spoke up and addressed the subject herself.

"I'm cool with the hidden fish and with the stickers as long as we use them as active reminders of what we are trying to create and what is at stake if we lose it. I think we should flash our fish at patients and families as a way of showing them our approach to patient care and, more important, as a way to generate more of these conversations we have been having. They will ask us what it means and we will have to explain what we are doing in our own words. Every time we do that, we will clarify what really matters to us and recommit. Does that make sense?"

There was a general outpouring of excited agreement. Rhonda made a decision on the spot.

"You guys are fantastic. I have not shared some of the things I have been doing, although I have shared my overall concerns. It appears we all are concerned about sustaining our way of working. So I want to tell you what I have learned, and what I still hope to learn, from a sushi chef."

There were a number of open mouths when she said *sushi chef*. But she decided to continue. "I don't think we can afford the time away from work to involve everyone directly in the beginning, so I would like to suggest we form a task force of volunteers representing the different shifts and different wings."

A Team Is Formed

Rhonda was pleased that Ping, Beth, Chad, and several others volunteered to join the task force. Their first meeting was held two days later at 3:30 p.m. in the break room.

"Thanks for volunteering. I know that with workloads what they are, you are making a real sacrifice. I've arranged for one hour of overtime for those who are on the day shift and for those who offered to stay late and cover for the volunteers on the evening shift. I know it's not much, but it may buy a bad cup of coffee in the cafeteria.

"A friend introduced me to a woman who operates a sushi restaurant called Takara Too, in the city. The conversations all of us here have been having about work were her idea. She has offered to meet with a group of us on a day when the restaurant is closed to share some of the ways they maintain their unique customer experience; one that has New Yorkers lined up each night in the cold, waiting for a chance to experience it.

"Her qualifications are simple. Her family business in Seattle has been in operation since 1950. It has remained a favorite there by changing with the times but always keeping the focus on the customers. For example, when tempura started to lose its appeal and tastes changed toward sushi, they adapted without missing a beat or losing a patron. The place we will meet, Takara Too, has had a long line outside every evening for four years. I believe we can learn something about keeping our vision alive from Ishy, the top sushi chef and co-owner."

"Rhonda."

"Yes, Justin."

"It's a restaurant. We're a hospital."

"That's true. And I've thought a great deal about that. But remember where we got the idea for the way we work on six. We learned it from a bunch of fishmongers. Remember: *That's* why we've had all the fish stuff. You can't always predict where you will find wisdom. We didn't want to *be* fishmongers; we were inspired by the possibilities we saw in their life at work. By the way, does anyone know of any research done during our implementation of ideas inspired by the fishmongers?"

Heather spoke up quickly. "I'm working on my MBA at NYU and we were assigned a yearlong team research project. My team was fascinated with the program and chose to look at the changes here on our ward. We created a survey and interviewed patients and staff. We also analyzed data that is routinely collected by the hospital on subjects including turnover and length of stay. Actually, we were in the middle of collecting the second round of survey data when you were promoted."

"Really! I don't remember being interviewed or filling out a survey. I must be getting old."

"You weren't randomly selected."

"Oh. I like that explanation better than getting old. Do you have any results?"

"We have a first draft of the report. I'll get you a copy."

"How does it look?"

"Our instructor suggested the results were highly significant."

"Good or bad significant?"

"Good significant."

"That might be useful information to pass along to Miss Scallpell. Now let's do some planning."

By the time the allotted hour had passed they had agreed on a date for representatives of the team to visit Takara Too.

Sushi for Nurses

The group assembled at Takara Too and was joined by Ishy, her husband, Hiro, and one of her staff. Rhonda recognized the staff member as Tako of Diet Dr Pepper fame. Introductions were made and everyone settled in. Ishy had prepared a special hand roll for everyone. You could see that Chad, one of the male nurses on the team, was fascinated.

"This is a Special Family Roll. Here, take some, Chad. In 1950 my grandfather and grandmother and two great-aunts decided to open a restaurant. They were by nature lighthearted and caring people, and the restaurant took on those qualities as well. At first it was an extension of the family. As we became successful, we needed to add non-family members, and it was also time for my grandparents to retire. We were faced with the challenge of maintaining the place for which we had become well known. We didn't want to lose it with the retirement of my grandparents.

"My father was a physician who worked long hours, and so it was pretty much up to my mother to figure out what to do. She would go for long walks, visiting successful merchants along the way and always asking lots of questions. Over time and with many mistakes our recipe for renewal evolved.

FIND IT

"My mother realized that a high level of commitment is always present in a strong and healthy organization. She began talking with her employees about the ideals to which they were committed. She discovered they had a lot more energy during and after discussions about values and commitment. She learned that talking about their commitments served to strengthen and clarify them.

"So what are you committed to? Let's start with you,

Chad, since you seem to be especially enjoying the hand rolls."

"Am I eating too much?"

"There is an endless supply, Chad. What are *you* committed to?"

"Well, to the vision and mission of Good Samaritan of course."

"And what is that?"

"You know; the stuff on the card. I haven't memorized it or anything, but I sort of know what it is."

"That stuff on the card is written to communicate with a broad range of people. How have you personalized it?"

"I am not sure what you mean."

"How have you translated that broad vision to your own working life?"

"Well, I'm committed to being part of the quality in *quality patient care*. And I want my contact with patients to be compassionate, intelligent, thoughtful, and lighthearted, rather than stiff, distant, or distracted."

"Well said, Chad. And even though you haven't memorized the Good Samaritan vision, you've found your place within it."

"Yeah. I guess I have."

FIND IT

The most basic ingredient of any vision is the individual IT.

IT is our personalization of the vision.

Vision-sustaining energy is released as we seek to find our IT through conversation.

"Anyone else?" asked Ishy, as she began preparing spicy tuna rolls.

"I'm committed to supporting my colleagues at work," added Kathy.

"I'm committed to choosing an attitude that enhances the work environment," mumbled Justin with his mouth full.

Tako spoke up. "It might help for me to explain what happens here from my perspective. We all have different roles and we will often talk about the tasks we do and how to do them better. Most places do that, I think. What is different here is that we also talk about the experience we are working to create by the way we do our work. We think about who we are *being* while we do the work we are *doing*. I wait tables; Ishy and Hiro make sushi; and other staff members perform other functions. But while we do different things, together we create an experience by the way we engage our customers and each other in the process. We talk about how we can create a unique experience every day that will draw our customers back for more."

Ishy nodded to Tako and continued, "That is the kind of discussion you need to have frequently to keep a vision energized. A few weeks ago, I suggested that Rhonda return to Good Samaritan and start a series of deep conversations about work. I understand you have started talking this way about work and you have already seen a change in the energy level. That's not surprising. My mother found the same thing thirty years ago.

"It's in the search for your special connection to the vision, and your conversations with each other about that connection, that your commitment becomes real. To contribute to keeping a vision alive and well you must first find your IT inside the vision. A formal vision is created for many constituencies but you draft your IT just for you. The conversations you have started support you in your discovery and rediscovery of your IT.

"You might want to consider a regular meeting where you talk about your commitments and exchange ideas about your IT," suggested Ishy. "My sister has continued to have regular meetings and frequent conversations at Seattle's Takara. And we have them every week here. It's hard to have these conversations on the fly, so you need to carve out special time together."

LIVE IT

Ishy continued. "Finding your IT is the starting point, but not enough in and of itself. More of the actual staying power comes from the next step: living your IT."

"Living it?" Mallory asked.

"Yes. So much of what happens in any thriving organization is spontaneous creativity fueled by a strong commitment to a vision. When you commit to something big, you see opportunities you might otherwise miss. You are open to them. It sounds a bit fuzzy at first, but we all commit to the vision of Takara Too and understand that we recreate it every day by the way we live at work. It is not just the work we do—which is to make and sell great sushi. It is also who we are *being* while we do the work we do."

"I'm not sure I understand what you mean by seeing things you might otherwise miss," remarked Ping.

"What I am referring to are opportunities to live the vision. But why don't I let Rhonda describe what happened the first time she and Margo came to the restaurant."

Rhonda made circles out of the fingers of her hands and held them up to her eyes like glasses. "Margo forgot her reading glasses and we were handed menus at the door. Margo returned hers because she couldn't read the small print. Literally seconds later the host was standing next to us with a whole tray of reading glasses of different strengths. It was, like, wow."

Ishy went on, "Each day we are presented with many

vision moments, or opportunities to reinforce or creatively extend our vision of the Takara experience. The more we act on these opportunities, the stronger the Takara experience becomes."

"I think I have an example from my life as a mother," said Rhonda. "I want to nourish a love of words in my children. So whenever I come upon a new word I get excited and we take some time to find out what it means. My children are now doing the same thing on their own. My stepdaughter, Ann, who had learning difficulties as a child, has developed an extensive vocabulary. The vision is to become lovers of words and the vision moments are new words that show up. It becomes an adventure."

"That's a good example, Rhonda. You've committed to raising educated children. That commitment allowed you to see an opportunity to nourish a love of words. The vision moments arise when new words present themselves and you transform the learning of these new words into adventures. Does anyone have a nursing example?"

All heads turned when the very quiet and shy Heather started to speak. "I watched Juan do something yesterday that really impressed me. We had an elderly man who came to us from ICU after a major stroke. His wife was rather creaky, needing a four-pronged cane to ambulate,

LIVE IT

Once we are clear about our IT, opportunities to Live IT are more obvious.

We call these opportunities *vision moments.*

Vision-sustaining energy builds as we live as many *vision moments* as we can.

and she was planning to stay overnight with her husband. It would have been hard on her.

"Juan sat down with her and took her hand. He told her how her husband now had a larger family including all of the staff on the floor and how we were dedicated to taking good care of him. Then he turned his collar to expose a small plastic fish. He said the staff wore that fish to remind them that this man is now a special member of the hospital family and will be treated accordingly.

"She went home to her own bed, much to the relief of her son and daughter. Juan took the time to put her mind at ease and also saved the night staff from the extra work that would have come from having this woman in the room all night. I think Juan saw a vision moment."

"That's it exactly," said Ishy. "Seeing opportunities to *be* the vision leads to the recreation of the vision every day. Each of you is responsible for recreating Good Samaritan each day from scratch by the way you live there. You are it. You are Good Samaritan. So 'Live IT.'"

Ishy went on as she prepared another kind of sushi. She said, "Find IT and Live IT are critical, but without the last element of the recipe it's still just a matter of time before any vision fades. This last ingredient is both important and difficult."

Justin said, "I'm all ears."

Ishy smiled and apparently decided not to say exactly what had come into her mind. Justin did have rather large ears.

COACH IT

"Most of the time here at Takara Too we are pretty good at living the vision, but we are human, we make mistakes, and we have times where we lose our focus. That's why the final element is so critical to our overall performance. We call our method of keeping one another on target *coaching*. After all, the job of a coach is to help you do your best.

"Here, everyone becomes a coach, and any one of us can coach anyone else. It doesn't make any difference how much seniority you have or where you are on our very short ladder. In fact, I get coached all the time."

Tako leaned forward and spoke. "I was hired a couple months ago, replacing a member of the waitstaff who decided to return to Japan. During the interview process they told me about coaching and I thought to myself that I would believe it when I saw it. I was happy to have the job, so it wasn't a big thing to me, but I was curious.

"One day Ishy brought a piece of tuna back from the

market and I looked at it and saw a light discoloring that I had seen once before. Sometimes that color pattern indicates that the tuna is not really fresh. I told Ishy that, and she looked me in the eye and said, 'Look, if I didn't think it was fresh it wouldn't be served.' She spoke with an unusually harsh tone. I don't know why, but I challenged her by saying I didn't think a curt response to coaching was in the spirit of what we had discussed in the interview. I was sure I would get fired.

"Ishy actually blushed and apologized. She told me I was right and her tone was inappropriate. We then talked about my experience, and Ishy listened while I told her my theory about what happens when salt gets on the ice while fish are being transported."

Tako looked down at his feet and continued. "It's great to be able to exchange views about things that are factual or experiential. But what started as coaching about stuff became coaching about the way we treat each other and I was afraid I had stepped over the line. Now I see that the fact we can have those real conversations not only helps make this a great place to work, but it helps us create the Takara experience every day."

Ishy smiled. "Tako is being kind. My first thought when he told me the fish might not be fresh was that I have been buying fish my whole life and I certainly would not buy a tuna that was not fresh. However, I answered with an attitude that was inappropriate, even if I had been correct. As Tako coached me about my attitude, the tuna became less important because the very spirit of coaching was under the microscope. We have all committed to listening before deciding whether we will accept or reject coaching. So I listened and learned. And I think the fish was fresh."

They all chuckled at the final comment. Then Beth spoke up. "The other day I allowed the negative spirit of another nurse to affect me and I was living outside the vision for a moment. Rhonda overheard me referring to a patient in impersonal and critical terms and she called me on it. She was absolutely right. I guess I was being coached."

"You were definitely being coached, Beth. How did it feel?"

"Well, my first response was to feel a bit defensive. We work in stressful conditions and it was just one time I slipped up. But Rhonda reminded me of what we were trying to create on our floor, and I support that vision of what work can be. In a way it was about the vision, not just about me. But I did get busted!" At this Beth smiled at Rhonda, who nodded agreement.

COACH IT

Coaching is a gift we give to each other and to our vision to keep IT strong.

Whether it's about the way we do our work or the way we work together, the feedback needs to flow in all directions.

Coaching can't be an ego trip. We only do it for the vision. We Coach IT.

Ishy went on. "Coaching is evidence that you have taken your responsibility seriously, because it's hard to coach. Coaching is done by those who are deeply committed to making the place great, not just good. You demonstrate your commitment to the vision by coaching. You also demonstrate your commitment by allowing others to coach you. Coaching is the glue that holds us together and the fuel for the little corrections that keep a place burning bright. And coaching can be the stimulus for the little innovations that reinvent us.

"When you are new or are unsure of something, you need to ask for coaching. When you are an old-timer you need to share your experience by coaching. But the old-timer may have routines that keep him or her from seeing new possibilities. So when you are an old-timer you also must be open to coaching. Giving and accepting coaching is the final demonstration of your commitment to the vision. Commitment is an abstraction by itself. **Find IT, Live IT,** and **Coach IT** are the actions that make commitment real."

"Someone is pounding on the door," Chad interrupted. But by then all were aware of the knocking, and the door was opened to expose a shocked and disheveled-looking Will Bullock.

Rhonda ran to the door asking, "What is it, Will?" Will said he had news that was too awful for the phone— that he had to come tell Rhonda in person. Rhonda was immediately at his side and again, in a softer voice, said, "What is it, Will?"

Will looked at her through wet red-rimmed eyes and said, "Ann is dead." Between sobs he could be heard saying something about a car accident and a drunk driver. For a long while they just held each other. Then a friend of theirs who had been standing just outside helped them to a car that had been parked awkwardly at the curb. They drove away.

When you work at a hospital, you are familiar with death. That doesn't make it any easier when it is one of your own. In this case, all of Rhonda's coworkers and new friends were experiencing the vicarious shock of a parent's worst nightmare. They stood in stunned silence, a few silently weeping. After a while, Ping said that she was going to call the hospital. That broke the spell and they slowly drifted away to find the comfort of family and friends. Ishy remained behind, her head in her hands, her husband's hand on her shoulder.

A Parent's Worst Nightmare

We expect some day to lose our parents—but no one expects to lose a child. It violates the natural order of things. And when you are young, you give no thought at all to the prospect of losing an older sister. It was devastating for Mike and Mia. Both of them had worshiped Ann.

At the hospital the shock waves spread outward in all directions. But the reaction that surprised everyone came from Miss Scallpell.

Two hours after Ping had called with the awful news, a cab pulled up to the Bullock residence and Miss Scallpell walked up to the door. When a man with a neatly trimmed gray goatee answered she asked, "Is this the Bullock residence?"

"Yes, it is, but this is not a good time."

"Are you Will?"

"No, I'm Will's brother. Are you a friend of the family?"

"I work with Rhonda at the hospital. May I speak with her, please?"

"I'm sorry. I seem to have lost my manners. We're all in shock here. Please come in. Who shall I say is here?"

"I'm Mable Scallpell."

"Please sit down."

Mable looked around the room. It was like sitting in a photo gallery. She could quickly identify Ann. In one lovely picture Ann was standing beside a famous actor. Ann looked so vibrant in the picture.

"Miss Scallpell. What are you . . . ?"

"Rhonda, I'm here to help. I've helped out like this before"—*and it was done once for me*, she thought—"and I know what to do."

"But you don't have to . . ."

"Nurses throughout time have supported one another at times like this. You have your grieving to do and arrangements to make. I will see that the phones are manned and the table is set with food. If there is anything else you need just let me know. I'm so sorry, Rhonda. I know there aren't words, but I want you to know I am here to do whatever you need done. I have experienced loss in my life and I want to be here for you. I will stay in the background, but ask me for whatever you need."

With a *thank you* Rhonda returned to the family room, where she was sitting in shocked silence with Will. Occasionally a desperate wail would fill the air followed by uncontrolled sobbing.

I remember all too well, thought Miss Scallpell. *Something like this stays with you for a lifetime.*

Miss Scallpell went into action. In thirty minutes she had arranged around-the-clock teams of nurses to prepare food, answer the door, go to the airport, run errands, shuttle guests, make beds, do dishes, and screen phone calls. When members of the gospel choir arrived with food and offers of help, they were quickly integrated into the team. This continued until the day after the funeral, when Will and Rhonda left for a memorial service organized by Ann's friends in LA. The last thing Miss Scallpell and the volunteers did was clean the house from top to bottom.

Back at the Hospital

The work of a hospital demands constant attention, and in this case the rhythm of work was a welcome escape from the harsh reality of what had happened to a friend. When a colleague loses a child, everyone realizes that it could just as easily have happened to him or her.

A touching note was posted on the bulletin board, dictated by a six-year-old girl with a head injury—a trauma that could have been prevented with the use of a seat belt. This young girl, struggling to regain her own life, sensed something was going on and asked about it.

When she heard about Rhonda's loss she insisted on writing a note.

> *Dear Nurse Rhonda*
> *You might not remember me but I am the little girl in 611.*
> *I am very sorry your daughter died.*
> *It makes me sad.*
> *You must be sad too.*
> *I would like to give you a hug when you return.*
>
> *Love,*
> *Tena*
>
> *P.S. If I have already gone home I won't be able to give you a hug.*

Ping and Beth met in the hall. "You know, Beth, there are so many good people and so much kindness on this floor . . ." She couldn't finish the sentence.

"I feel it too, Ping. When something like this happens it makes you reflect on how you are living and what life is all about. We can so easily become mechanical in our work, but at a time like this our compassion comes to the surface. It feels like we become a little softer around the edges. That's why we need to keep our philosophy of work alive. That's why we became nurses: to be human. I've been thinking about Rhonda's return. I've heard it takes months before she'll have what might even remotely be called a normal day. Maybe we need to continue what was started at Takara Too. None of us wants to see a return to old ways; life is too precious to live that way at work. The best way we have to honor Ann's memory is to continue what Rhonda has started. We are on the way to renewing the lighthearted, compassionate, conscious way of working."

"You know, we spend more time at work than we do with our family and friends. We spend more time here than we spend in our places of worship. We spend more time at work than we spend in nature. The largest portion of our time spent awake is spent here. This is also an opportunity to test our commitment, to prove that it can be about much more than simply having more fun at work."

"Good afternoon, ladies."

"Miss Scallpell."

"I see those silly little fish are out in the open again."

"Well, we . . ."

"I may have acted a bit hastily when I first arrived. I have been looking at some data that Phil and I received from Heather and while it is preliminary, it is dramatic. You should be proud. I heard so many good things about this place when I was at the corporate office, but I really had no idea of the source of those good things. The progress in patient and staff satisfaction on this floor has been remarkable.

"But my original point remains. Are you doing anything to make sure you sustain the gains you have made— or is it just becoming a lot of distracting window dressing that hides real problems?"

"Well, we . . ."

"You know, when Rhonda comes back she will do her job and do it well, but I don't think you can continue relying on her to lead cheers."

"We were just talking . . ."

"I enjoy these talks. It's good to be back with nurses giving care. So enough chitchat, eh?" And Miss Scallpell turned to leave.

"Miss Scallpell."

She turned back to look and said, "Yes, Ping."

"Thanks for all you did. We were all wondering how to help Rhonda and her family, and you organized it all and made sure we were doing the things that were actually needed."

For the first time Miss Scallpell seemed to be at a loss for words. Her eyes began to glisten. Finally she said, "Nurses stick together, and I have had some experience with sudden loss: My husband died suddenly, many years ago. When Rhonda returns, she will not be upbeat and full of fun, but she will still be a fine nurse. There are times when melancholy is appropriate. And remember that Rhonda is on a different time line from the one we are on. Rhonda will experience intense moments of sadness for years, and that is the way it should be.

"Her grieving doesn't mean she cares less about the fun environment you have worked so hard to install here; life is not always up and she is simply being fully human. Now is your chance to prove that what you are doing here can incorporate the full breadth of human emotions and personality types—that it really is all about being committed to the patients and each other—that it's not just about fun." With that she left, pulling a handkerchief out of a heavily starched pocket as she walked away.

Beth looked at Ping. "She may be from another generation but underneath all that stiff white material is definitely the heart of a nurse."

The Memorial

Rhonda and Will arrived in Los Angeles with red-rimmed eyes and an empty feeling in their hearts. Ann's roommate, Jill, boyfriend, Rob, and friends Greg and Melissa had organized a memorial service on the beach near where Ann and Jill lived. It was a section of beach known for its regular appearance on *Baywatch* and for the dozens of volleyball courts found there.

Rhonda and Will arrived, parked their car, and looked out at the beach, where about eighty people were already standing around two blazing fire pits.

"I'm not sure I can do this, Will."

Will looked lovingly at his wife as they sat in the rental car. "You don't have to do anything, sweetheart. Do you want me to take you back to the hotel? These are her friends, they will certainly understand."

"Where do you get the strength?"

"You give me too much credit. Right now I am simply trying to get from one minute to the next. But these were her friends and I know so little about her life in the LA film business, even though she was out here for years. I want to hear about the Ann that her friends and coworkers knew."

Rhonda opened the car door and stepped out. "That's a wonderful way to approach this memorial. We will celebrate this part of her life." Rhonda took hold of Will's hand and they walked to the beach.

A Plan Forms Back at Good Samaritan

"So let's make it easy on ourselves, Beth. Let's divide into three groups based on our primary ward assignment, and each group will take one of the three principles described by Ishy. I will work with the renal wing and tackle 'Find IT,' if that's all right with you."

"That's fine, Ping. Our wing will take 'Live IT' and Chad can take 'Coach IT.'"

"How will we describe the task? I know our goal is to keep our great work environment alive, vital, and evolving. But how do we frame things?"

"Let me take a shot at that, Beth. I think our primary task is to further educate ourselves about the commitments, to share what we have learned in a fun way that involves the others, and to invite our colleagues to come up with specific ideas we can put into practice here—ways to create vision moments."

"Oh, Ping. I made some copies of the notes I took at

Takara Too. I'll brief Chad on our plan when I give him his copy. And one more thing . . . Is this OK? I mean, do you think Rhonda will mind? You know, that we are taking things into our own hands."

"Actually, I think Rhonda will be relieved. She has felt such a heavy personal responsibility for continuing what started under Madeleine's watch. I now see that we can and should take part of that burden."

There are three principles that guide Takara Too as they sustain the remarkable Takara experience.

Find IT *A vision is often designed to serve multiple constituencies. A vision comes alive only when it is personalized by those who work in the vision community. This happens when each of us assumes responsibility for finding our IT inside the vision. And we can only find our IT through conversation with other members of the vision community. The employees of Takara Too regularly take the time to talk about the place they want to create and the role each of them has in that creation.*

Live IT *Every day we are presented with countless opportunities to recreate the vision. Ishy calls these* **vision moments.** *Once we have found our IT we must commit to living IT by living fully the naturally occurring vision moments.*

Coach IT *Keeping a vision alive is hard to do alone because it is difficult to observe yourself in action and feel the impact you are having on others. Therefore feedback plays a key role. By creating an atmosphere where it is not only OK but our responsibility to give and receive feedback, we will make the daily adjustments necessary to keep the vision strong. This is called coaching and it is a crucial ingredient in sustaining anything worthwhile.*

Note to self:
We all must discover the power and importance of these ideas for ourselves and choose to enroll of our own free will. Natural energy comes with personal choice.

Return to Takara Too

A month had passed since Ping and Beth had their planning conversation on the sixth floor. Rhonda had returned to work but was clearly affected by her tragic loss. She could often be seen just staring into space. It seemed to help her to be actively involved in direct patient care, and so the staff frequently asked for her help in challenging cases, for which she was now showing an even greater aptitude than she had before. Rhonda took special interest in the slow but steady progress of little Tena in 611 on the children's neurology wing; Tena's letter had a prominent place on Rhonda's bulletin board alongside a picture of Ann.

Rhonda and Miss Scallpell were briefed on the plan and were delighted. Phil had stopped by to indicate how excited he was with their effort and offered his help.

Miss Scallpell, as usual, had a lot to say. Ping, Beth, and Chad were becoming accustomed to these one-sided conversations and were actually beginning to enjoy them. It was during one of those conversations that Miss Scallpell suggested a lunch meeting to which she invited Rhonda, Ping, Beth, and Chad. They were asked to meet outside her office at 11 a.m.

"This is a bit early for lunch, isn't it?" asked Chad as he stood outside Miss Scallpell's office with Ping and Beth. Miss Scallpell emerged in a rush and they found themselves scrambling to keep up as she took off through the revolving door at the main entrance and headed for the parking lot.

"Shouldn't we wait for Rhonda?"

"She decided to cover things here for the three of you."

"That feels weird," said Chad.

"Understandable and professional," Miss Scallpell responded crisply as they marched down an aisle. "You are the team leaders, are you not?"

"Yes, but . . ."

"Enough said, hop into my car."

"Where are we going?"

"The city."

The car turned quiet as they crossed the George Washington Bridge and headed downtown. Comments were generally about the passing view. In New York, the people-watching is world class. Finally Ping asked, "So what's up for lunch, Miss Scallpell?"

"I'm an eye blink away from retirement and I spend a lot of time thinking about leaving a legacy. I am quite proud of the research programs I established for the system and thought I might coast through my last two years spreading old-fashioned nursing wisdom to a new generation of nurses. I wasn't prepared for what I found at Good Samaritan. The opportunity we have here is enormous.

"Heather's research validates what you already knew. Your efforts have had a major impact. But what I saw when I arrived was an overreliance on the externals and an inability to integrate new people. You've taught me a lot. I hope I've taught you something too. Now let's see if this much-discussed sushi chef can tell us the rest of what we need to know. Well, here we are." Miss Scallpell managed to find a parking place a short walk from the restaurant.

Ishy and Margo were waiting for them as they emerged from the car. They held open the plastic curtains used to protect those waiting in line each night from the elements.

"I can taste the sushi now." Beth was almost drooling.

Ishy smiled and responded, "Actually, we ordered corned beef sandwiches from the deli down the street. Just kidding! I have both."

They sat down at a long table and the sandwiches were passed around along with an elegant tray of sushi.

Margo spoke first. "Some of you may know that I have been active in a city-wide leadership program where I was lucky enough to meet Ishy. What you may not know is that Mable is a founder and past president of the organization."

The three nurses looked at Miss Scallpell with a mix of disbelief and respect.

"So it's not surprising that we talk to one another frequently, since what we have in common is a concern for Good Samaritan and for my oldest and dearest friend, Rhonda. Rhonda and I go back to first grade, you know.

Ishy and I want to be sure you all are getting the support you need. How are the teams doing with their assignments?"

Ping glanced at the other two nurses, who nodded, and then spoke. "Actually it isn't going well at all. We understand about the importance of finding your IT inside the vision, but we are not sure how to get started. Maybe some examples from other organizations would make it clearer.

"And we have some ideas for helping people understand 'Live IT,' and some specific vision moments to cite, but we are having trouble thinking of a way to actively engage the staff. A list of steps would be helpful.

"And, yes, 'Coach IT' is the most straightforward of the three. We know people will understand honest and clear communication because we have a tradition of feedback in health care; we have patient-care audits and medical reviews. But how do we develop a habit of choosing the same honesty and authenticity in our conversations about the way we work and who we are being at work? Again some more examples might help us."

Ishy responded, "When Rhonda went back to the hospital after our first meeting together, her plan was to begin talking to people about their work and what they wanted to get from work."

"Yes," said Ping. "I remember the day Rhonda asked if we could talk about the way we work. At first I thought I had done something wrong. That discussion led me to talk with Juan and see how we had let him down by not being more thoughtful about his need to get integrated in our way of working."

"And I understand you experienced a surge of energy as you began talking about work at a deeper level."

"It was amazing how quickly that happened."

"Well, you must have faith in that natural energy. It is always available if you can make the conversations real. And you don't really need any more examples."

"We don't?"

"I don't think so. You seem to understand the principles and you have seen how we do what we do. The time for understanding has passed and now is the time for action."

"By the way," said Miss Scallpell, "I've talked to Rhonda and she wants to get involved again, but she is concerned about stealing your thunder. She is really impressed with the way you three took responsibility and made a commitment to keep things moving. She doesn't want to interfere."

"Interfere!" Ping said. "Her interest in getting more involved in the project is the best news I've had in a long time. But let's get back to Takara Too. Can you give us some pointers on things to do to get started? Do you have like a list of things to do? I mean these ideas originated in your family business, didn't they?"

"I think I would phrase it another way," said Ishy. "Takara and Takara Too discovered the commitments needed for sustaining a vision, but we did not create them. They have been around for a long time. Ping, it's time for action.

"Your implementation strategy must be crafted in a way that respects your culture at Good Samaritan. I deeply appreciate your recognition of our efforts here, but you must find your own way of bringing this wisdom to life in your world. To spend any more time watching us or analyzing the things we do would only distract you from your real work. Your real work is to bring these commitments to life at Good Samaritan."

"We just aren't sure what to do."

"That's because your journey is unique. You may be using a set of ideas that are as old as time, but your application is brand-new and has to be discovered by you. Action in the face of the unknown requires some courage. More examples and more study is a natural but problematic form of resistance to action.

"The philosopher Joseph Campbell helped me understand. He said if you see your path laid out in front of you Step One, Step Two, Step Three, you only know one thing for sure: It's not your path. Your path is created in the moment of action. If you can see it laid out in front of you, it means you can be sure it is someone else's path. That's why you see it so clearly.

"I've learned to be open to any inspiration that comes from observing effective organizations at work, but when it comes time to take action, the last thing I need is to borrow someone else's 'how to' list. What I need to do is to take my own first step.

"We have nothing more than sushi to give you now. It is time for you to take the step that does not yet exist. You must create it."

And so they all sat at the table for another hour talking and becoming more comfortable with the inevitability of the task ahead: finding the one path that is theirs and theirs alone.

Chad and Beth walked to the subway station and left Ping and Mable to fend for themselves. They wanted to compare notes. While they were deep in conversation a store window caught Beth's attention. They stopped for a minute to study the array of family pictures on display.

Once guiding principles are understood, it is time for action.

We think we need to find the one well-worn trail that others have followed and that it will take us where we want to go.

The truth is that we must blaze our own trail and all we will ever have as a compass is a set of commitments and our faith.

"I guess people have always captured the special moments in their life. I wonder how they did it before photography?"

"They drew pictures on the cave wall of course. What is it, Beth? You seemed to drift away there for a moment while you were looking at this display. What are you thinking about?"

And Beth shared the idea that had been stimulated by the photogaphs. Then, recognizing the deep exhaustion they both felt, they decided to take a cab all the way back.

The Commitment Gate: Find IT

On Monday morning, five weeks after Ishy issued her action challenge, the FISH! STICKS project made its first public move. In the lobby of the sixth floor at Good Samaritan, a picket fence with an old-fashioned hinged gate had been erected, but it was labeled *Commitment Gate*. Above the gate was a sign with two questions.

Are you committed to the vision of Good Samaritan?
Have you found your IT?

Off to the side was a one-chair information center and standing in front of elevators were Ping and a member of her Find IT team along with Rhonda and Miss Scallpell. As staff came off the elevator or through the door they received a big smile, a greeting, a printed card, and a silly pin.

On the back of the card was the latest version of the hospital vision statement with some new text as well.

Are you committed to the vision of Good Samaritan? Have you found your IT?

On the back of this card is a copy of the Good Samaritan vision statement. It is an important public statement of our commitment to quality health care and a great work environment, and it is written in general language for a variety of stakeholders. But it remains words on paper until you and I commit to finding our place inside the vision and bringing the vision to life through our work and through the person we are being while we do our work.

An upbeat, lighthearted, and team-based approach to work developed here on the sixth floor. The quality of our work life and patient care benefited greatly from this way of working. But now we must decide if we are committed to sustaining this expanded vision of our work. Our first step must be finding our individual IT inside the vision so we can choose to live IT. And there is only one way to find our IT: through real conversations with colleagues about work.

We hope you are willing to demonstrate your commitment by having at least five conversations in the next two weeks. These conversations should provide clarity about your IT. The questions below are meant to be a starting point for each of the conversations.

🐟 When in your workday do you know you are living the vision?

🐟 What is the experience we are trying to create for patients and staff?

🐟 How do you personalize the vision?

🐟 How can we support each other in keeping our way of working alive and vital?

By 8:30 a.m. most of the staff working the day shift had seen or played with the Commitment Gate and received a smile, the greeting, the card, and the pin. The last to visit was Phil, the hospital director.

"That seemed very effective," said Phil. "But what's the deal with the pins? I thought we were moving to a more internal energy."

"We are," answered Miss Scallpell. "The external devices can only take you a certain distance and we all agree about that. But I've realized that symbols and ritual serve an important purpose in keeping a vision alive. I read about the power of symbols and rituals in a *Harvard Business Review* article about the Ritz-Carlton and I saw a connection. Let me ask you a question, Phil.

"What happens when a patient, family member, or someone from the outside sees an unusual pin on a nurse's lapel?"

"Well, I suppose that person might be curious."

"Exactly. And what happens when you begin answering their questions?"

"I get it. When you answer questions you clarify and reinforce your own understanding and your commitment. The pin assures the conversations continue by stimulating them. What else do you have up your sleeve?"

"Well, I think the Commitment Gate will be here for a few weeks. And I think we need a lost and found for those who have lost or have never found their IT. Then there is the idea that came from the planning team."

"And what would that be?"

"Where to put Miss Scallpell's starched hat, of course," Rhonda chimed in, pointing to the side of the gate, where one of Mable's hats was being hung on a special hook by Ping, Beth, and Chad. "That's a reminder to us on the sixth floor of how much Miss Scallpell has given us. Any chance you might consider delaying that retirement, Miss Scallpell?"

Photographic Memories: Live IT

The flyer announced a contest open to the staff on the sixth floor. The rules were simple. Each team would have a section of the lobby reserved for that team and a bulletin board to display photographs taken by the members of their group who were caught in the act of living their IT. These photos of vision moments would be mounted on the bulletin boards. The rules also indicated that the boards could be decorated, and that all the photos needed to be of vision moments where a hospital patient wasn't physically present. And all had to be true snapshots—not posed. The teams would have four weeks to prepare the displays. A committee of nurses from other floors would judge the results.

> ## "Live the Vision"
> ## Contest Announcement
>
> All members of the sixth-floor staff are invited to participate in the first annual Live IT competition. The purpose of this contest is to identify and portray the many ways we live the vision of Good Samaritan each day by living our personal IT. You are invited to form teams based on your work assignment and to compete for the prizes.
>
> It is the task of each team to capture spontaneous *vision moments* in photographs. *Vision moments* are those times when we are living the vision of Good Samaritan. The pictures will provide a documentary of the moments you and your team bring to life in the course of your work, and will be displayed for judging. See the detailed rules on the back of this flyer and contact Beth at 6121 with any questions.
>
> Good luck!

First prize was on display. It was a picture of a giant tray of sushi. The real sushi would go to the winning team.

The Live IT Judging

Four weeks had passed since the contest was announced and the lobby was packed. "I hope the fire marshal doesn't show up," said Beth jokingly to Juan.

The spokesperson for the selection committee moved to the small stage that had been erected and took the microphone. Silence fell over the crowd, which included representatives from all the teams.

"Ladies and gentlemen, it is my pleasure to announce the Live IT winners and present the awards. The instructions were to create a collection of photographs depicting the many ways our vision is personalized by those who work on and support the sixth floor. It was the hope of the contest organizers that the search for the ways we live the vision, or *vision moments*, as we now call them, would make us all more aware of the opportunities we each have every moment of every day to keep our precious vision alive and full of energy. May I have the envelope, please?"

Margo stepped up and handed her the envelope. "This is Margo Carter, executive vice president of Eastern Bank Systems, where the results have been locked in the bank vault." There was polite laughter, but everyone seemed ready for the results.

"Second prize goes to the very competitive team from top management. The judges were especially impressed with the amount of 'play' that goes on in the executive suite. The vision moments where senior executives are meeting with and listening to groups of employees over lunch was also a factor in the decision. I understand they had to eat in the cafeteria because the executive lunchroom was full of pictures." There were some chuckles. "Give them a hand."

Phil stepped up to accept the prize but declined making any remarks with the quiet comment, "I don't want to detract from the main focus, but I do want to announce that the executive lunchroom will reopen as a general purpose room for everyone's use. This idea came from our own Miss Scallpell, who convinced me that doctors, nurses, and other staff often need a place to get away for a minute or two." This comment received a well-deserved hand.

"And now for the first prize. This was an easy decision for the judges. First prize is awarded to the nurse assistants and nutritionists of the sixth floor. The selection committee was impressed not only by the array of things you captured in your pictures as you do the work that is at the heart of our mission at Good Samaritan, but also by the example you set for the rest of us.

"Your collection of pictures about everything you do behind the scenes for patients made its point so clearly thanks to the clever way you approached it. We especially liked the pictures of the food trays for pediatrics with the pancakes decorated to look like Pokémon characters. It was a powerful statement of how simple it is to create a higher quality of life for those we serve just by spending a little extra time and ingenuity. You've given new meaning to the phrase, 'play with your food.' We will be displaying your pictures on a rotating basis in all parts of the hospital, and they will then go on a tour of all the hospitals. And we're even going to turn the photos into a slide-show video for the kids and staff.

"An anonymous donor has provided a gift basket for each of you. This person is doing this to demonstrate his thanks to you for the wonderful care you gave his wife while she was on six. Good job!"

Coach IT

The Coach IT team had gone underground and Chad was not talking to anyone about what they were doing. Two weeks after the vision moments were on display, Ping tracked him down.

"How is it going, Chad?"

"Just fine. Good seeing you, but I've got to run."

Later Beth encountered a shrug and a polite, "Chill out," when she inquired about the progress of the Coach IT team.

Rhonda, who was taking a more active role as time passed, was especially concerned. She knew that all three ingredients were important and that without coaching, the vision was at risk.

On Friday morning, three weeks after the awards ceremony, Rhonda received a call from Miss Scallpell. The call was received with pleasure. Miss Scallpell had become a friend and mentor and Rhonda had no doubt it would be a sad day when she retired. *What a change since my first encounter with Miss Scallpell,* she thought.

"Rhonda. Would you come down to Phil's office?"

"Sure. What's happening?"

"Nothing urgent—but do come to Phil's office if you aren't busy."

"I'll be right there," said Rhonda.

"Thanks for coming down," said Phil. As soon as Rhonda set foot in his office, she was given a small stack of cards, elegantly hand-lettered.

"Chad has been working overtime with his team and

it took them a while to figure out something to do," began Phil. "Now I'll let Chad explain how he envisions us putting the cards to use."

"Here's the deal," said Chad. "When it comes to coaching there is no recognition of hierarchy or seniority. We all have the same responsibility: to coach without reference to position and to receive coaching without discrimination. We also have the right to accept or reject the coaching we receive.

"Coaching is not an ego trip but a responsibility we each have to help keep the vision strong. Coaching will keep the conversations real and help us make work a reward and not just a way to rewards.

"We are now going to the sixth floor to start a weeklong coaching effort. Each of us will explain what's on the card to one other person and then give that person the whole rest of our stack of cards. They will need to do the same—but each person has to find a new person to receive their remaining stack, someone who hasn't been given a card before.

"Take a look at the cue card and see if you have any questions."

COACH IT CUE CARD

🐟 Have you enrolled in the vision of Good Samaritan and begun the search for your IT?

🐟 Are you willing to accept coaching from anyone who has an idea that might help you better live the vision?

🐟 Are you willing to coach others?

🐟 Do you acknowledge each person's right to accept or reject the coaching?

🐟 Will you ask for coaching when you need it?

🐟 Can you think of coaching examples from your work? (Make this a two-way exchange.)

🐟 Are you ready to become a part of the Coaching Crew?

🐟 Now it is your turn. Take the rest of this stack of cards and give it to one other person. Keep one card.

🐟 Be sure to share your own coaching stories with that person and ask him or her to do the same.

🐟 Good Luck!

They were off to the sixth floor. Within three days, everyone on the floor had received a card.

The End?

And the vision at Good Samaritan is still alive today. It lives one conversation, one vision moment, and one coaching session at a time. The model established on six served as a base from which the principles spread throughout the hospital and then throughout the hospital system. There is no question that initiating a significant change is difficult and satisfying. But when the change you worked so hard to achieve begins to fade, the ultimate challenge appears: sustaining that change as the gravity pull of old ways of being starts to exert itself. This is when the long-term winners claim the ultimate prize. Getting change to STICK!

FIND IT
LIVE IT
COACH IT

And enjoy the benefits of your hard work for a long time.

FISH! STICKS

Postscript

A visit to Good Samaritan today finds most of the usual characters still present. Rhonda has developed into an outstanding director of nursing. She misses Ann terribly, but she is also aware of Ann's legacy. Rhonda has a much deeper sense of compassion for her patients and colleagues; that part of her IT has expanded. Phil and Madeleine are now at corporate together. They frequently bring groups to Good Samaritan for insight and inspiration but not to give the groups a "to do" list. "It is time to act!" Ping exclaims at the end of each session.

If the groups get back on the bus mumbling about the need for more examples—a form of resistance that Madeleine and Phil have become experts at handling—the two of them help them with questions and probing comments so that these new groups can chart their own way and create their own special vision moments.

Juan is a lead nurse now and is frequently sought out for his ideas and expertise. And whenever people on the staff venture to Takara Too, they come back complaining about the line they had to wait in outside and marveling at the experience they had inside.

And there is a new poster on the walls:

We have discovered that the secret to keeping our vision alive in today's challenging work environment is for each of us to commit to finding our IT inside the vision, to living IT, and to coaching IT.

Many people talk about the importance of commitment, but commitment remains an abstraction until we take action. We demonstrate our commitment by taking the following actions:

FIND IT LIVE IT COACH IT

DEDICATION

On November 12, 2000, I was packing my bags and about to leave for Turkey when the call came that every parent dreads. A coroner in San Bernardino asked if I had a daughter Beth, and then proceeded to tell me that Beth Ann Lundin had been killed in the early hours of the morning on a desolate stretch of highway between Las Vegas and Los Angeles. She was thirty-one years old and she was living her dream in Hollywood, where she worked as a set designer. Her life ended in the amount of time it takes a drunk driver to lose control of his car. A drunk driver who then drove away and left her to die in a ditch.

You search for something to hang on to in such times: a picture, a memory, a story. There was no shortage with

Beth. She lived life to its fullest and the stories were many. The one I have chosen to share in this dedication I heard at her memorial service, which was held on the beach at sunset in Playa del Rey, California. As we assembled with her friends to celebrate her life, a young man came up and introduced himself. He said he had only known Beth for one short production, but felt that after the five weeks he knew her better than he knew many people he had worked with for years. He said she was always talking about this strange-sounding book that her dad had written, *FISH!* When she died he bought and read *FISH!* and he wanted to tell me that Beth lived the principles of FISH! He said, "Beth *was* FISH!"

There is a hole in my heart and an empty space in my life. I often wear her birth ring when I speak and feel that her spirit is with me when I talk about her vibrant brand of life. Beth's candle burned brightly on this earth, and in the early morning hours you can still see the glow on the horizon. After all, she was FISH! I love you and miss you, Bethy. You are my teacher and my inspiration.

S. L. (Dad)

Acknowledgments

There are many who have worked to make this book a success and we want to recognize them all, fully knowing we will probably miss someone. First we will acknowledge the special people and then single out four for extra recognition.

You couldn't ask for a better publisher. It seems unfair to the industry that Hyperion should have so much superior talent. Included on the fantastic team with whom we had the privilege to work are:

Bob Miller, Martha Levin, Ellen Archer, Jane Comins, Michael Burkin, Mark Chait, Jennifer Landers, Claire Ellis, Andrea Ho, David Lott, Vincent Stanley, and thanks also to the awesome Time-Warner Trade Publishing sales force.

And how did we get so lucky as to find the world's best agency? The Margret McBride Agency includes an all-star cast:

Jason Cabassi, Donna DeGutis, Sangeeta Mehta, Kris Sauer.

There would not be a book if it weren't for the incredible Pike Place Fish. Thanks to Johnny Yokoyama, the owner, and the amazing fish guys for creating and sustaining a world famous fish market.

And then there are the accomplished authors and business leaders who have shared their wisdom and their words. It is such an honor to have these talented individuals offering their support:

Sheldon Bowles, Richard Chang, Peter Economy, Peter Isler, Spencer Johnson, Lori Lockhart, Bob Nelson, Robert J. Nugent, Hyrum Smith, Donald D. Snyder, Richard Sulpizio.

We want to thank the employees of The Ken Blanchard Companies and ChartHouse Learning for the many little gestures that add up to a whole lot of help.

And we would like to recognize four people who made major contributions:

Our editor, Will Schwalbe, brought enthusiasm, experience, and a willingness always to be looking for ways to improve the book, right down to the last minute.

Patrick North of ChartHouse offered his Mobius Award–winning talent.

Ken Blanchard offered his guidance and wrote a wonderful foreword.

Finally, the agent of all agents, Margret McBride. For a writer, she is a treasure.

Thanks.

Stephen C. Lundin

Harry Paul

John Christensen